KU-157-723

Drugs and crime: the results of research on drug testing and interviewing arrestees

by
Trevor Bennett

A Research and Statistics Directorate Report

Home Office
Research and
Statistics
Directorate

London: Home Office

Home Office Research Studies

The Home Office Research Studies are reports on research undertaken by or on behalf of the Home Office. They cover the range of subjects for which the Home Secretary has responsibility. Titles in the series are listed at the back of this report (copies are available from the address on the back cover). Other publications produced by the Research and Statistics Directorate include Research Findings, the Research Bulletin, Statistical Bulletins and Statistical Papers.

The Research and Statistics Directorate

The Directorate consists of Units which deal with research and statistics on Crime and Criminal Justice, Offenders and Corrections, Immigration and General Matters; the Programme Development Unit; the Economics Unit; and the Operational Research Unit.

The Research and Statistics Directorate is an integral part of the Home Office, serving the Ministers and the department itself, its services, Parliament and the public through research, development and statistics. Information and knowledge from these sources informs policy development and the management of programmes; their dissemination improves wider public understanding of matters of Home Office concern.

First published 1998

Application for reproduction should be made to the Information and Publications Group, Room 201, Home Office, 50 Queen Anne's Gate, London SW1H 9AT.

©Crown copyright 1998   ISBN   1 84082 069 1
                         ISSN   0072 6435

Foreword

There has been considerable speculation in recent years as to the proportion of crime that is drug-related. This report, based on research in five English locations, gives a clear assessment - based on urine testing - of recent drug consumption on the part of samples of people arrested by the police. It also illuminates, through interview data, a wide range of related issues, including the extent to which acquisitive crime is committed to fund the purchasing of drugs.

The research was carried out for the Home Office by the University of Cambridge, broadly along the lines of an established programme in the United States.

DAVID MOXON
Head of Crime and Criminal Justice Unit
Research Statistics Directorate

Acknowledgements

I would like to acknowledge those people who helped in conducting the research. These include the Home Office for funding the project and Malcolm Ramsay for his advice and assistance in designing and implementing the research. They also include the chief officers and area commanders in the selected police force areas for agreeing to host the research. Special thanks are due to Stuart Lockhart for managing and conducting the fieldwork throughout the project; Jonathan Smith for co-ordinating and conducting the fieldwork for part of the project; and the other researchers who worked as interviewers at different stages in the research. Special thanks also go to the staff in the various custody suites for their considerable support. I would like to acknowledge the help of the Home Office Forensic Science Service at Chepstow (formerly at Aldermaston) in giving advice on procedures relating to specimen collection and drug testing. Thanks are also due to the project secretary (Gail Bennett) and the administrative and library staff at the Institute of Criminology. Finally, I would like to acknowledge the assistance of academic and DUF Program contacts in the United States who have provided helpful advice on research issues and the operation of the DUF Program.

TREVOR BENNETT

Contents

Summary

In 1987, the National Institute of Justice in the United States launched a programme of drug testing of arrestees called the Drug Use Forecasting Program (DUF). This programme involved trained staff conducting quarterly surveys of all arrestees in booking facilities in initially 12 and later 23 large cities in the United States. At the end of its first decade of operation, the programme was relaunched under the name of the Arrestee Drug Abuse Monitoring Program (ADAM) and will soon be expanded to 75 North American cities. The combined programmes have resulted in the publication of a large amount of unique and high-quality information about the nature and trends in drug use in the United States and its links with criminal behaviour.

There has been no similar programme conducted in England. No previous research has attempted to drug test samples of arrestees and very little other research has been conducted on drug use among arrestees. Consequently, very little is known about the prevalence of drug use among this group and very little is known about the links between drugs and crime in relation to arrestees. The current research was established just over two years ago (in January, 1996) with a view to rectifying this situation by developing research in this country, similar to the DUF Program in the United States, based on interviewing and drug testing arrestees.

The research sites

In total, surveys of arrestees were conducted in five police force areas over the two-year period of the research. The first survey was conducted in Cambridge at the Cambridge City custody suite which is the main designated custody block for the Southern Division of Cambridgeshire Police Force area. The second and third surveys were conducted in Hammersmith in London and in Trafford in Manchester. The fourth survey was conducted in Nottingham City Centre Division of Nottinghamshire Police Force area. The fifth survey was conducted in Sunderland City Division of Northumbria Police Force area.

Methods

The current research design is based on the methods used in the DUF Program. However, it was necessary to adapt the methods to suit the conditions relating to the processing of arrestees in Britain. In total, 839 arrestees were interviewed across the five research sites and 622 of these (74%) provided a urine specimen. The achieved response rates across the five survey areas varied slightly as shown below:

• proportion of detainees approached who were interviewed: 83%-87%

• proportion of detainees interviewed who provided a urine specimen: 63%-82%

Eight drug types were tested in relation to each of the five surveys:

• cannabinoid metabolite

• opiates (including heroin)

• methadone

• cocaine metabolite (including 'crack')

• amphetamines (including ecstasy)

• benzodiazepines

• LSD

• alcohol

Prevalence of drug use

The urinalysis results showed that the average rate of positive tests across all locations, excluding alcohol, was 61 per cent. The equivalent rate including alcohol varied between 72 per cent and 82 per cent of arrestees depending on location. The most common drug identified was cannabis (46% tested positive) followed by alcohol (25%), opiates (18%), benzodiazepines (12%), amphetamines (11%), cocaine (10%), and methadone (8%). No arrestees tested positive for LSD. In a number of ways, these percentages represent very high rates of drug use among a broad range of arrestees.

A breakdown of the results shows that for most drugs females were as, or more, likely to test positive as males. Females were significantly more likely than males to test positive for opiates and higher percentages of females than males tested positive for methadone, cocaine, amphetamines, and benzodiazepines (although these differences did not reach statistical significance). Older arrestees (aged 21 or more) were more likely than younger arrestees (aged 16 to 20) to test positive for opiates, methadone, and cocaine.

These high drug-use prevalence rates among arrestees are also reflected in the estimates of the prevalence rate of drug use in relation to particular offence types. The research showed that almost half of arrestees suspected of shoplifting across the five survey areas tested positive for opiates and about one-third tested positive for cocaine. About ten per cent of all suspected burglars and one-quarter of all suspected car thieves tested positive for opiates.

Drugs and crime

The current method of drug testing and interviewing arrestees was designed primarily to identify prevalence rates of drug misuse. It was not designed to test whether there was a causal connection between drug use and crime (which would ideally require repeated surveys over time and more detailed questioning and data collection than was possible within the current research design). Nevertheless, some of the data collected could be brought to bear on the issue.

Almost half of arrestees (46%) who reported using drugs in the last 12 months believed that their drug use and crime were connected. The most frequent connection cited was the need for money to buy drugs. There was also some support for the view that arrestees whose drug use and crime were connected would report higher levels of criminal involvement. Arrestees who said that their drug use and offending were connected reported illegal incomes (a measure of criminal involvement) on average two to three times higher than those who said that their drug use and crime were not connected.

The research found a statistically significant correlation between number of positive urine tests and amount of reported illegal income (the average illegal income of arrestees with no positive tests was £3,000, compared with over £12,000 among arrestees with three positive tests). Arrestees who tested positive for opiates, methadone, or cocaine reported levels of illegal income two to three times higher than those who tested negative for these drugs.

A multivariate model showed that the best predictors of illegal income were reported use of heroin or crack. A 'what if' analysis was conducted to see the effect of reducing the illegal income of arrestees who reported heroin and/or crack use to the level of those who used neither heroin nor crack. The results showed that illegal income for the sample as a whole would be 32 per cent lower. If the consumption of heroin and crack were wholly responsible for this differential, then removing these factors from the equation would result in a reduction of criminal involvement among this sample of arrestees by as much as one-third.

Injecting drugs

All arrestees who reported that they had consumed at least one drug type in their lifetime were asked if they had ever injected one of four drugs (heroin, methadone, cocaine, and amphetamines), plus any additional drugs, ever, in the last 12 months, in the last month, and in the last three days. The results show that 19 per cent (1 in 5) of all arrestees admitted injecting at least one illegal drug at some time in their lives. Fourteen per cent of arrestees reported injecting drugs in the last 12 months. The results vary slightly by type of drug. Thirteen per cent of arrestees said that they had injected heroin in their lifetime and 1 in 10 of all arrestees said that they had injected heroin in the last 12 months. Approximately 1 in 10 arrestees said that had injected amphetamines in the last 12 months and 1 in 20 arrestees said that they had injected cocaine.

Almost one-third of arrestees who had ever injected illegal drugs had shared a needle at some time in their lives. Three per cent of the total sample said that they had shared needles in the last 12 months (22 per cent of all arrestees who had injected over the last 12 months). The main reasons given for sharing needles were the absence of clean needles, the convenience of sharing, or the belief that there was no health risk.

Drug dependency and treatment

Just under one-half (45%) of all arrestees said that they had been dependent upon one or more drugs (excluding alcohol) at some time in their lives. Almost one-third (30%) of all arrestees said that they were currently dependent upon one or more drugs. Eleven per cent of arrestees said that they were dependent upon heroin at the time of arrest. Two per cent of all arrestees said that they were currently dependent upon cocaine and three per cent said that they currently dependent upon crack.

One in five arrestees said that they had received some kind of treatment for drug dependence in the past and about the same proportion said that they would like to receive treatment at the current time. A small proportion of arrestees said that they preferred some form of maintenance or stabilised prescribing of the drugs of their addiction. However, a larger proportion of arrestees said that they wanted help in coming off drugs (7 per cent in Sunderland and 9 per cent in Nottingham). The remainder wanted other kinds of help including counselling and individual or group therapy.

Discussion

The study has identified a number of key findings which might need to be addressed in the future. The main finding is the high prevalence rate of drug use among arrestees. The research also raises issues relating to problems relating to health, drug dependency, and lifestyle. Overall, the research draws attention to the overarching problem that, with some notable exceptions, arrestees come into contact with the criminal justice system and are released again (either immediately or eventually) without any of these issues being addressed.

The research concludes by encouraging policy makers to consider developing a arrestee monitoring programme (and associated research capacity) in this country. It is argued that arrestee monitoring can provide a large number of potential benefits, including:

• an alternative measure of drug use among a high-use population over time and across different geographic areas;

• a means of providing information which can help generate local-level profiles of drug use and which can be used to inform intervention strategies;

• a method of predicting changes in the rate of crime (through known correlations between drug use and crime) or seriousness of crime (through additional information on use of weapons and the nature of the drugs-crime link);

• a means of evaluation for local programmes which have attempted to prevent or modify in some way local drug use.

I Introduction

Introduction

For the last ten years, the United States has implemented a large programme of research based on interviewing and drug testing samples of arrestees. The programme was originally called the Drug Use Forecasting Program (DUF), but recently has changed its name to the Arrestee Drug Abuse Monitoring Program (ADAM). The programme was extensive (covering shortly after its inception 23 large cities and soon to be expanded to cover 75 cities) and was generously funded by the National Institute of Justice (NIJ). The aim of the programme was originally to 'forecast' drug misuse by monitoring short-term changes in the prevalence of arrestees testing positive for a range of drugs using urinalysis. However, the research data have been used to generate a much broader picture of drug use across the nation, including trends in drug use, variations in the distribution of drug use, changing drug use preferences, and a wealth of information of the characteristics of drug use and drug users.

At the time of the first discussions about the current research, in the mid 1990s, almost nothing substantive was known about drug use among arrestees in England. There was a widespread belief, based largely on anecdotal evidence and some 'best guesses', that the prevalence of drug use might be high. There was also some concern that there might be a connection between drug use and crime and that some proportion of all crime could be attributed to drug use. However, there was no substantive research on the subject that could provide a valid estimate of the actual amount of drug use among arrestees. This situation of limited information in an important area of drug use encouraged some researchers and policy makers to consider whether the apparent successes of the DUF Program in the United States could be repeated over here.

The Home Office commissioned the Institute of Criminology to conduct a feasibility study to determine whether it would be possible and useful to interview and collect urine specimens from arrestees in custody suites in England. The report to the project concluded that it was feasible and much could be gained from developing such a programme in this country

(Bennett, 1995). The findings of the feasibility study provided some support for the broad principles of current government policy outlined in the White Paper, 'Tackling Drugs Together: A Strategy for England'. The White Paper expressed a need to generate good-quality indicators of drug misuse and to develop research on the connections between drug misuse and crime as part of the wider strategy relating to the treatment and control of drug misuse. Shortly after the submission of the report, the Home Office Research and Statistics Directorate agreed to fund the second stage of the research which would pilot a programme of interviewing and drug testing arrestees.

The aims of the research were: (1) to develop a procedure for interviewing and drug testing arrestees based on the DUF Program in the United States which be could be used in police forces in England; (2) to generate an alternative measure of drug use through urinalysis which might usefully supplement existing measures of drug use; (3) to generate information about the prevalence of illegal drug use in the survey sites of the selected police force areas; and (4) to consider what drug testing and self-reported interviewing of arrestees can contribute towards understanding the relationship between drug use and crime.

The Drug Use Forecasting Program (DUF)

The research was strongly influenced by the procedures and general approach of the DUF Program in the United States. The DUF Program began in New York City in 1984 with a feasibility study based at the Manhattan Central Booking Facility. The research was funded by the National Institute of Justice (NIJ) and was conducted by staff from the Narcotic and Drug Research Incorporated (NDRI). As part of this research, NDRI staff interviewed and obtained voluntary urine specimens from recent arrestees. The aim of the study was to demonstrate that it was possible to obtain urine specimens from arrestees being processed in large urban booking facilities. The authors concluded that the project was successful in achieving its objectives and in generating high response rates. Ninety-five per cent of arrestees approached consented to be interviewed and 84 per cent of these provided a urine specimen (Wish and Gropper, 1990).

In September 1986, the researchers returned to the Manhattan Central Booking Facility to obtain specimens and conduct interviews with a second sample of male arrestees. The second survey was also successful in achieving similarly high response rates from among the arrestees. However, the study was also successful in another unexpected way. The timing of the study was in a sense fortuitous as between 1984 and 1986 New York City experienced a substantial increase in the use of cocaine (especially 'crack' cocaine). The study detected this and showed that the prevalence of cocaine use among arrestees almost doubled over the two-year period from the first to the second survey (42% in 1984 to 83% in 1986). The results of the comparison were striking and identified a trend in cocaine use over a year before it was detected by any of the other indicators of drug misuse (e.g. new treatment admissions, overdose deaths, and emergency room admissions) (Wish and Gropper, 1990).

In 1987, the NIJ established the DUF Program in 12 large cities across the United States. This was soon expanded to 23 adult sites and 12 juvenile sites. Throughout this period to the current time, DUF staff have conducted quarterly surveys of arrestees held in the booking facilities covering the research sites. The data are collected and analysed centrally by DUF staff at NIJ who publish quarterly and annual reports of the results. The reports contain prevalence trends of the percentage of positive tests for arrestees for each DUF site for three of the ten main drug types analysed (cocaine, opiates, and marijuana), along with 'any drug' and 'multiple drugs'. The early reports included breakdowns of the urinalysis results in terms of age, sex and race of the arrestee and more recent reports have included additional breakdowns based on the type of charged offence.

The Arrestee Drug Abuse Monitoring Program (ADAM)

In 1997, the National Institute of Justice launched a new programme called the Arrestee Drug Abuse Monitoring Program (ADAM) which succeeded the DUF Program. It is intended that the new programme will maintain the principles of the DUF Program, but will be tripled in size to cover up to 75 urban areas and will be expanded to include more detailed local data collection NIJ (1997[a]). The National Institute of Justice also plans to develop an international programme called the International Arrestee Drug Abuse Monitoring Program (I-ADAM) which is a research partnership among criminal justice organisations around the world. The main aims of I-ADAM are to extend the principles of the DUF and ADAM Programs in order to generate a better understanding of drug use and the connection between drug use and crime across countries. It also aims to provide a basis for sharing information which might help in developing effective policies (Riley, undated).

The research design

The current research design is based on the methods used in the DUF Program. However, it was necessary to adapt the methods to suit the conditions relating to the processing of arrestees in Britain. At the outset of the research, a large part of the procedures to be adopted were untried and untested in this country and it was not known how the procedures might be best designed in practice. Hence, the research strategy was to sample a number of research sites over a period of time with sufficient time allowed between each survey to reflect on the methods used and to adjust them if necessary.

In total, five surveys were conducted in five police force areas over the two-year period of the research. The first survey was conducted in Cambridge at the Cambridge City custody suite which is the main designated custody block for the Southern Division of Cambridgeshire Police Force area. Cambridgeshire was chosen as the first research site as it was the local force for the research project. It was thought important during the early developmental stages of the research that the force was friendly to the research aims and was forgiving of any errors that might be made. The time allowed to conduct this part of the research was four months (January to April 1996), which was longer than the other surveys in order to allow time to develop the methods.

The second and third surveys were conducted in Hammersmith in London and in Trafford in Manchester. These sites were selected (during a process of discussion with representatives of these and other forces) with the specific aim of including police force areas which might have sites within them with drugs problems. The research design established in Cambridge was used in London and Manchester with little change, with the exception that the data collection period was reduced from four months to two months (July to August 1996).

The fourth survey was conducted in Nottingham City Centre Division of Nottinghamshire Police Force area. The main aim of selecting Nottingham was to identify a police force area which had a moderate drugs problem and was a provincial rather than a metropolitan force. The methods used for sampling arrestees was changed in the Nottingham survey and departed from the DUF model of 'convenience' sampling. The revised system was a form of 'probability sampling' and involved 24-hours-a-day, seven-days-a-week interviewing (see the next chapter for more details on the sampling method). The data collection period for the survey was reduced to one month (January 1997). In addition, the questionnaire used for the interviews in the fourth and fifth survey was revised to include a number of additional questions.

The fifth survey was conducted in Sunderland City Division of Northumbria Police Force area. The main aim of the site selection for the last survey was to find an area which had a relatively low drugs problem. We were also interested to sample a police force area in the north of the country in order to provide some geographic spread. The eventual choice was (once again) a combination of our decisions and the decision of representatives of the police forces in which we were interested. The revised sampling methods and the larger questionnaire developed in Nottingham were repeated in Sunderland. The survey period was also reduced once again to a single month (July 1997).

Hence, the research involved a process of development of the procedure for selecting and interviewing arrestees. The selection of police force areas was based on what appeared to provide the best balance in terms of research design. The final sample of five police force areas thus represents a spread across metropolitan, urban, and partly rural forces, a spread across southern, midland, and northern forces, and a spread across forces in terms of the level of their drugs problems.

Despite the developmental and evolving nature of the research design, each of the five surveys can be shown to be representative of the population of arrestees from which they were drawn (see Appendix A). Nevertheless, it should be borne in mind that the population investigated effectively changed after the third survey from dominantly day-time arrestees to all arrestees processed during all hours of the day. It is estimated that under-sampling evening and overnight arrestees in the first three surveys had the effect of underestimating drug use prevalence (Bennett, 1997a;1997b).

The structure of the report

The report focuses mainly on the results obtained from the five surveys. However, because of the uniqueness of the methods used in the current research and because of the importance of the methods in understanding the nature of the results obtained, the next chapter of the report discusses the methods used in some detail. The third chapter provides the main findings of the research concerning the prevalence of drug use among arrestees in each of the five sites. The fourth chapter uses information from the urinalysis results and from the interviews to examine the links between drug use and crime. The fifth chapter examines the issue of injection of drugs among arrestees and the important health issue of needle sharing. The sixth chapter examines drug dependency among arrestees and their treatment needs. The seventh chapter includes the findings of the lifestyle addendum and covers issues relating to gun ownership, AIDS, hepatitis, living conditions, and involvement in the criminal justice system. The final chapter discusses the results and considers their implications for policy relating to drugs and crime and the treatment of offenders.

2 Methods

Introduction

The current research is based closely on the methods used in the DUF Program in the United States. However (as noted above) the research design was adapted to the British system of processing arrestees.

Sampling

In the DUF Program sites, arrestees are not selected using the more common method of probability sampling (i.e. a system of sampling whereby the probability of each person in the population being selected is known or can be calculated). Instead, arrestees are selected at the discretion of site personnel who are guided by a target sample size and a crime charge priority system (NIJ, 1996). Hence, the selection process is sometimes described as a 'convenience sample' rather than a random sample. The system of non-probability sampling is justified in the DUF literature on the grounds that the often chaotic nature of booking facilities does not lend itself to systematic random sampling. Detainees are approached as they become available. Known sources of sample bias are reduced as far as possible through the system of quota controls. It is also argued that this is not a critical issue as long as data-collection procedures remain the same at each measurement point (Wish and Gropper, 1990).

This method of sampling was chosen for the first three surveys (in Cambridge, London, and Manchester). There were two main reasons for choosing convenience rather than probability sampling for the first three surveys: (1) it was not thought possible within the early stages of the research to operate a system of sampling which required a tight control over the research environment, as we were still learning about the nature of this environment and what was possible to accomplish within it; and (2) we accepted the advice given in the DUF literature that it would not be feasible 'under the often chaotic nature of booking facilities' (Wish and Gropper, 1990) to conduct any kind of probability sampling in which the researcher told the police who was going to be interviewed.

However, there are various problems with convenience sampling. The main problem in relation to the current research was that it allowed interviewing to be conducted at the discretion of the interviewer. In practice, this resulted in the majority of interviews being conducted during day-time hours and during weekdays. An analysis of the population and sample data for the three force areas showed that the sampling method tended to under-select detainees who had been arrested in the evening and overnight (Bennett, 1997a; 1997b). The method also tended to under-estimate the drug and alcohol involvement of the sample compared with the population of all arrestees. Hence, it was decided to attempt some form of probability sampling (despite the fact that it had never been done within the DUF Program).

The method chosen to achieve this was to use four researchers working three shifts a day in order to provide 24-hour cover for seven days a week. Every detainee passing through the custody suite during the research period had a known and equal chance of being selected. In essence, the population and the sample were the same and each arrestee had a probability of '1' of being selected. In practice, it was necessary to exclude certain groups of detainee as ineligible for inclusion in the sample prior to selection (see the next section for details of inclusion criteria). However, this adjustment did not undermine the principles of the approach as the selected sample was representative of a known and identifiable population of detainees (i.e. those eligible for inclusion).

Eligibility

The DUF Program operates a system of sampling which excludes certain categories of arrestee as being ineligible. One condition was that arrestees had to be in custody for less than 48 hours. Other conditions related to the kinds of offences for which the detainee was arrested. The conditions of eligibility used in the current research excluded the following categories of arrestees.

- Detainees who were unfit for interview due to alcohol/drugs/ medication

- Detainees who were considered mentally disordered

- Children and juveniles

- Detainees who would require an interpreter

- Detainees who were considered to be potentially violent

- Detainees who had been in custody in excess of 48 hours

- Detainees who were deemed ineligible for other reasons at the discretion of the custody sergeant or gaoler

The research included both males and females and all ethnic groups as eligible for interview.

Sample size

The target sample sizes in this research were based on DUF Program recommendations. In the United States, approximately 225 males and 100 females are selected for interview in each survey. It has been argued that using this number produces a fairly representative sample and attempts to compare the characteristics of arrestees selected for interview and drug testing and the characteristics of all arrestees processed in the same site have tended to show a close correlation between the two (Decker, 1992). The target sample size for all surveys was set at 225 and (as probability rather than quota sampling was used) no separate targets were given for males and females. In practice, this target was not reached during the early stages of the research, but was exceeded in later stages of the research.

Data collection periods

On average, researchers working DUF sites in the United States spend 14 consecutive days at the central booking facility during each three-month period. It was noted above that the data collection periods in the current research shortened as the research progressed (reducing from four months to four weeks). It was found that the shortest survey period required to interview the target number of arrestees was 28 consecutive days. With the relatively lower numbers of arrestees per month in custody suites in Britain (in the region of 500 a month among our survey sites compared with many thousands a month in some booking facilities in the United States), it was not possible to achieve the DUF Program target of 14 consecutive days.

Achieved samples

The achieved sample sizes are shown in the following table (Table 2.1). In Sunderland and Nottingham a systematic procedure was used for collecting information about all arrestees processed during the survey period (in response to the revised system of sampling which required monitoring all arrestees as they were processed). In the final two surveys, there is full information on the total population, the total eligible and ineligible, and the sample sizes. In the first three surveys, (during the use of convenience sampling) systematic information was not collected on each arrestee passing through the custody block. Hence, the first four rows in the following table are not completed for these survey areas.

Table 2.1: Achieved samples in the five survey areas

Location	Sunder-land	Notting-ham	Cam-bridge	London	Man-chester	Total
Total detainees processed during research period	635	781	*	*	*	*
Total ineligible	238	375	*	*	*	*
Total eligible	397	406	*	*	*	*
Total detainees approached	311	246	180	*	*	*
Percentage of those eligible	78	61	*	*	*	*
Total detainees interviewed	271	209	152	103	104	839
Percentage of those approached	87	83	84	*	*	*
Total urine specimens collected	210 [1]	132	124	79	77	622
Percentage of those interviewed	77	63	82	77	74	74

Notes: [1] In one case, a laboratory test result was obtained, but the interview schedule relating to the case could not be traced. This case has been excluded from all analyses which require both sources of information.

The table shows that 61 per cent (in Nottingham) and 78 per cent (in Sunderland) of those eligible for interview were approached for interview. Eighty-seven per cent of arrestees in Sunderland and 83 per cent and 84 per cent respectively of arrestees in Nottingham and Cambridge approached for interview were interviewed. Over 80 per cent of arrestees in Cambridge who were interviewed agreed to provide a urine specimen and over 70 per cent of arrestees in Sunderland, London, and Manchester agreed to provide a specimen. A slightly lower specimen rate was achieved in Nottingham. The main reasons for losses at each stage of the sampling processes (including the reasons why certain categories of detainees were deemed to be ineligible from the outset) are discussed in detail in Appendix A.

Questionnaire

The questionnaire used in the research was based on the questionnaires used in the DUF Program (a combination of earlier and later versions). The main body of the questionnaire used in all surveys was divided into main sections covering the principal topic areas of the research including: self-reported drug use (ever, in the last 12 months, in the last month, and in the last three days); injecting drugs and sharing needles; dependency on drugs and alcohol; drugs and crime; legal and illegal sources of income; amount spent on alcohol and drugs; and treatment needs. The questions were mainly structured with pre-set response categories, although some were open-ended. The questionnaire was designed to be completed in less than 30 minutes. The questionnaire was revised slightly for the fourth and fifth surveys in line with revisions made to the DUF questionnaire (including additional questions on arrestee lifestyles).

Computer-aided interviewing

As part of the development of the research methods, some of the arrestees in the first three surveys were interviewed with the assistance of a computer. The questionnaire was designed on a software programme which had the facility for data collection during the interview using a lap-top computer. The main purpose of using the computer was to test out the method in order to determine whether there were any improvements in efficiency of data collection, compliance rates, or the validity of responses.

Two methods of using the computer were tried. In the first method, the interviewer read the questions to the respondent from the lap-top screen and entered the responses him/herself. In the second method, the interviewer gave the lap-top to the arrestee who read the questions from the screen and entered the response him/herself. In practice, it was found that few arrestees were sufficiently relaxed (having just been arrested) to concentrate on using a small screen and keyboard. There were also problems relating to the ability or the willingness of arrestees to follow the simple instructions required to enter the responses and move to the next page on the computer screen. Hence, in most cases in which a computer was used, the interviewer entered the responses him/herself.

The researchers noted a number of advantages to computer-aided interviewing. It was thought that it provided a focus for arrestees which helped them to become more engaged in the research. The novelty of using a computer-assisted and a 'technological' method of data entry was attractive to some of them. It was also argued that it gave an air of professionalism to the research which seemed to impress both the police and the arrestees. Arrestees also seemed to be reassured by the fact that the hinged screen which faced them rather than the door could be easily concealed should a police officer enter the room.

However, there were some disadvantages to using computer-assisted data entry which resulted in its relative lack of use in the current research. One disadvantage noted by the researchers was the loss of natural interaction at times when sensitive issues were being considered. Another disadvantage was the problem that the computer and the software took up some of the attention of the interviewer (especially at times of a computer malfunction or operator malfunction). Overall, it was decided that it would be safer to abandon the use of a computer and the final two surveys were conducted solely using paper questionnaires.

Drug-testing procedures

The current research is based on procedures for specimen collection and drug testing recommended by the Forensic Science Service (FSS). The DUF Program uses a 'chain of custody' procedure in order to ensure that urine samples are unadulterated and that test results are accurately matched to the people providing the samples (Wish and Gropper, 1990). A similar 'chain of custody' procedure was recommended by the FSS and was rigorously followed in the current research.

Arrestees were required to collect the urine sample in a specimen collection container and to hand this container to the researcher. The collection container had a heat sensitive strip on its side that registered (by the changes in the colour of indicator spots) whether the sample was close to body temperature (specifically whether it was in the range 90 to 100 degrees Fahrenheit). The contents of the collection container were then transferred to two sample vials in equal volumes. The lid of each vial was sealed and a security strip was placed across the lid and the base of the vial. Pre-numbered, bar-coded labels were then placed on the vials and both vials were placed in a sealed security bag.

The remainder of the chain of custody procedure was based on carefully completed documentation provided by the FSS which monitored the movements of the specimens and their conditions during transport. In most survey sites, the specimens were held in a refrigerator in a medical room in the custody block and later collected and transported through the local police carrier system for body samples directly to the FSS at Chepstow. The specimens were then stored in a cold store until they were ready to be tested.

Drug-testing methods

There are two main types of technology for drug testing. The first is collectively referred to as immunoassays and are used primarily for drug screening. The second is collectively referred to as gas chromatography and is used primarily for drug confirmation following screening. The former tests are less expensive and less reliable and the latter tests are more expensive and more reliable.

The main method used in the DUF Program in the United States is the immunoassay Enzymes Multiplied Immune Testing (EMIT) test. However, all positive results for amphetamines are confirmed by gas chromatography to eliminate positive results caused by over-the-counter drugs such as some allergy and cold medicines. The main method used in the current research was an immunoassay screening test, similar to the EMIT test, called the 'On-Line' Kinetic Interaction of Micro-Particles (KIMS) test. The choice of a screening test was based on a balance of its cheapness and acceptable levels of accuracy.

There are various factors which affect the accuracy of screening tests. The two main issues which have been discussed in the literature concern: (1) specificity (the ability of the assay to identify a single-chemical component in a mixture of chemicals and biological materials; and (2) cross-reactivity (the ability of a substance other than the drugs in question to produce a positive result). Screening tests are less powerful than gas chromatography in their ability to differentiate between drug types. It cannot differentiate cocaine and 'crack', amphetamine and methamphetamine, or among the various kinds of opiates. Screening tests are also less powerful than gas chromatography in guarding against other drugs, unrelated to (or chemically similar to) the drug under test, producing a positive result. Some over-the-counter allergy and cold medicines can produce a positive result for amphetamines and some codeine-based pain killers can produce a positive result for opiates (for further information, see Appendix C).

The issue of specificity could not be avoided and the research had to be based on what the KIMS screening test was able to deliver. This was a particular problem for the current study in relation to differentiating heroin and other opiates and 'crack' and cocaine. The issue of cross-reactivity was guarded against by asking all arrestees whether in the last three days they had used prescription or over-the-counter drugs and estimates of the likely error in prevalence figures resulting from this were calculated (the results are shown in Appendix C).

Drugs tested

Eight drug types were tested in relation to each of the five surveys: cannabinoid metabolite, opiates, methadone, cocaine metabolite, amphetamines, benzodiazepines, LSD and alcohol. A brief description of the drug groups is given below:

- *Cannabinoid metabolite*: a marker which identifies all forms of cannabis including its herbal and resin forms. Cannabis is usually classified as a hallucinogen.

- **Opiates:** the test identifies all forms of opium-based products including the pure compounds such as codeine and morphine and the semi-synthetic compounds such as heroin.

- **Methadone:** a wholly-synthetic opiate usually classified as an opioid. Its main legal use is in the treatment of heroin addiction.

- **Cocaine metabolite**: the test detects cocaine hydrochloride and is unable to distinguish the powder form, which is sniffed or injected, and the nugget form (crack), which is typically burnt and inhaled, as both metabolise in the body in the same way.

- **Amphetamines**: this group includes amphetamine sulphate, methylamphetamines, and similar amphetamine-like drugs such as 'ecstasy'. Amphetamines are usually classified as stimulants.

- **Benzodiazepines**: include all the minor tranquillisers such as diazepam and temazepam.

- **LSD**: lysergic acid diethylamide is usually classified as a powerful hallucinogen which is typically swallowed.

- **Alcohol:** includes all ethyl alcohol or ethanol-based products.

The approximate duration over which these drugs can be detected in urine varies slightly. It has been estimated (Wish and Gropper, 1990) that amphetamines are detectable up to two days after use; opiates, methadone, cocaine metabolites, and benzodiazepines are detectable up to three days, and cannabinoid metabolites are detectable up to three days from single use, up to 10 days with daily use, and up to 27 days from chronic use.

3 Prevalence of drug use

Introduction

This chapter presents the main findings of the report concerning the prevalence of drug use among arrestees. The concept of prevalence is used here to refer to the proportion of a population that has used drugs over a specified period of time. In this chapter, prevalence is examined over different periods of time (in whole lifetime, in the last year, in the last month, and in the last three days) and using different measures (urinalysis and self-reported drug use).

There are two main reasons for examining prevalence of drug use among arrestees. The first is that it provides a measure of drug use among a high-risk population. It has been argued that arrestees are likely to be the first group to begin using a new drug within a particular area and are likely to be more heavily involved in its use than the non-arrestee population. The second is that it provides an alternative measure of the correlation between drug use and crime. Previous research has aimed to assess the connection between drug use and crime by examining criminality among drug users and drug use among criminals (Bennett, 1991). However, most of this research has been conducted in the United States. In particular, there is comparatively little research in Britain on drug use among criminals and much of what has been done has been based primarily on prisoners. Almost nothing substantive is known about the prevalence of drug use in this country among arrestees.

Urinalysis

The use of urinalysis to measure the prevalence of drug use provides a more objective and more accurate measure of drug use within a population than self-report measures (issues relating to validity are discussed in Appendix B). The specimens collected during the interviews were tested by the FSS for eight drug types. The results were returned for each specimen stating whether each of the eight types resulted in either a positive test (the drug was detected) or a negative test (the drug was not detected). As most of the drugs tested (with the exception of cannabis) are detectable in the body up to three days following consumption, the results of the urinalysis effectively provides a prevalence figure of drug use within the last three days.

The results of the urinalysis relating to the five survey sites are shown in Figures 3.1 and 3.2 below.

The survey areas have been ordered in terms of increasing percentages of respondents who tested positive for multiple drugs. Overall, the charts show that most of the drug types follow this order of increasing prevalence across survey sites, with the notable exception of positive tests for alcohol, which tend to move in the reverse direction. Sites characterised by relatively high prevalence rates of positive tests for drug use are characterised by relatively low prevalence rates of alcohol use. The effect of a possible interaction between alcohol use and drug use can also be seen in the second of the two charts. The distribution of positive tests for 'any drug' is fairly flat across the five survey areas when alcohol is included in the calculation. When alcohol is removed from the calculation, the distribution of positive tests for 'any drug' forms into a strong increasing rank order across the survey sites.

The results shown in the figures are summarised and discussed below:

Figure 3.1 Percentage positive tests among arrestees for selected drug types

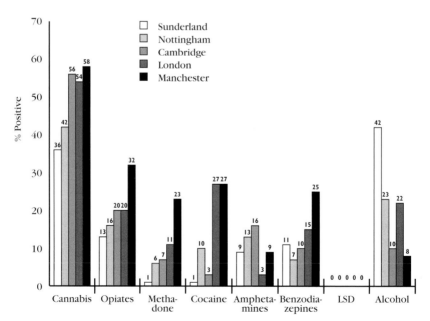

Note: The total for each area is the number of arrestees who provided a specimen.

**Figure 3.2 Percentage positive tests among arrestees for 'any drug'
and 'multiple drugs'**

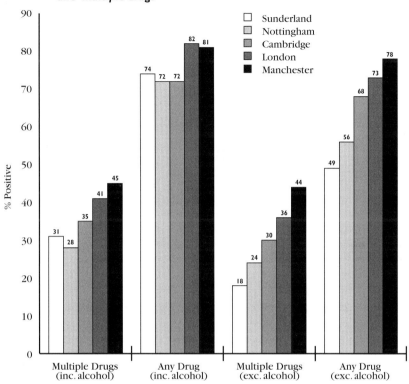

Notes: 'Multiple drugs' = 2 or more drug types. The total for each area is the number of arrestees who provided a specimen.

Cannabis: The proportion of arrestees testing positive for cannabis ranged from 36 per cent to 58 per cent across the five survey areas, with a median value (the midpoint of the range) of 54 per cent.

Opiates: The proportion of arrestees testing positive from opiates ranged from 13 per cent to 32 per cent with a median value of 20 per cent. The two metropolitan areas produced the two highest rates. It should be noted that some of these positive tests may have been produced by legally-prescribed or over-the-counter drugs such as codeine-based medicines.

Methadone: The proportion of arrestees testing positive for methadone ranged from one per cent to 23 per cent, with a median value of seven per cent. It cannot be determined from these tests whether the drug was legally prescribed (as an alternative to heroin in the treatment of heroin addiction) or purchased on the black market.

Cocaine: The proportion of arrestees testing positive for cocaine (or crack) ranged from one per cent to 27 per cent. The two highest prevalence rates were from the metropolitan sites. The median proportion of positive tests was 10 per cent.

Amphetamines: The proportion of arrestees testing positive for amphetamines, methylamphetamines, and amphetamine-like drugs including 'ecstasy' ranged from three per cent to 16 per cent, with a median value of nine per cent. It is possible that some of these positive tests were produced by legally-prescribed or over-the-counter drugs.

Benzodiazepines: The urinalysis showed that between seven per cent and 25 per cent of arrestees tested positive for this group of drugs, with a median value of 11 per cent.

LSD: No arrestees in any of the sites tested positive for LSD.

Alcohol: The proportion of arrestees testing positive for alcohol ranged from eight per cent to 42 per cent, with a median value of 22 per cent.

Any drug: The proportion of arrestees testing positive for any of the drug types tested (including alcohol) ranged from 72 per cent to 82 per cent, with a median value of 74 per cent. The effect of excluding alcohol from the calculation reduced the range to from 49 per cent to 78 per cent, with a median of 68 per cent.

Multiple drugs: Multiple drugs refers here to testing positive for two or more drug types. The proportion of arrestees testing positive for multiple drugs (including alcohol) ranged from 28 per cent to 45 per cent, with a median value of 35 per cent and the effect of excluding alcohol from the calculation reduced the range to from 18 per cent to 44 per cent, with a median of 30 per cent.

There are a number of observations which might be made in relation to the results shown above. The first is that, by a number of criteria, these figures represent high prevalence rates. Converting these percentages into approximate ratios leads to the following estimations:

- Three out of four arrestees tested positive for at least one drug (including alcohol)
- One in three arrestees tested positive for multiple drugs (including alcohol)
- One in two arrestees tested positive for cannabis
- One in five arrestees tested positive for opiates
- One in 12 arrestees tested positive for methadone

- One in 10 arrestees tested positive for cocaine

- One in 10 arrestees tested positive for amphetamines

- One in 10 arrestees tested positive for benzodiazepines

- One in five arrestees tested positive for alcohol

The second observation concerns the prevalence of positive tests among the arrestee sample and the prevalence recorded in other surveys. The following table (Table 3.1) shows the prevalence results of pre-arrest drug use found in related research. Each of the research studies provides fairly comparable findings over similar periods of time relating to samples of arrestees or prisoners.

Table 3.1: Pre-arrest drug use across selected surveys
Percentages

Drug Type	Prisoners	Arrestees	Arrestees	Arrestees	Arrestees
	Self-report	Observation	Various drug involve-ment indicators	Urinalysis	Urinalysis n=622
	England & Wales Maden et al. 1992 [1]	London Robertson et al. 1995 [2]	Manchester Chatterton et al. 1995 [3]	USA DUF Annual report DUF data 1995[4]	Five survey areas[5]
Alcohol	*	10 (22)	*	*	25
Amphetamines	4	*	*	1	11
Benzodiazepines	*	*	*	3	12
Cannabis	12	*	*	33	46
Cocaine	2	*	*	40	10
LSD	*	*	*	*	0
Methadone	*	*	*	1	8
Opiates	7	*	*	7	18
Any drug [6] (excluding alcohol)	*	*	19	65	61
Multi-drugs [6] (2 or more types excluding alcohol)	*	*	*	21	27

Notes: [1] Frequent use equivalent to use within 2 days of arrest;
[2] Figure in brackets includes drink-related offences;
[3] Including indicators of recent and past drug use and other kinds of drug involvement;
[4] Median value for adult males across 23 sites based on the published annual report (NIJ, 1996) and on additional calculations made on the archived data ;
[5] Mean values;
[6] Includes additional drug types apart from those shown above.

The first three columns compare the prevalence figures of drug use among arrestee samples in England and Wales using self-report, observation, and other methods (but not drug testing). The table shows that the current study based on five survey areas has higher prevalence rates for alcohol (when compared with the study of arrestees by Robertson et al., 1995) and for any drug (when compared with the study of arrestees by Chatterton et al., 1995). It also shows higher prevalence rates for cannabis, cocaine and opiates than the study by Maden et al. (1992) in relation to prisoners.

The fourth column compares the prevalence figures of drug use among arrestees across the 23 DUF sites for the year 1995. In terms of methods, this study is the most comparable to the current research as it is based on drug testing of arrestees. However, there are some differences in the way in which the DUF results and the current results are calculated which should be noted: the DUF results are based on median values and the current research results are based on mean values; the DUF results are based on adult male arrestees and the current research is based on both adult male and female arrestees; and the DUF method of urinalysis is based in some cases on slightly higher cut-off levels (the level at which the drug being tested is considered positive) than the urinalysis used in the current research. This latter difference might have the effect of deflating slightly (by a few percentage points) the DUF results compared with the English results.

The comparison of the two sets of results shows that in relation to each of the drug types, the percentage of positive tests is higher in the English sites than in the North American sites, with the exception of cocaine use and any drug use. The five English survey sites show higher rates of positive tests for amphetamines, benzodiazepines, cannabis, methadone, and opiates than the median values of the DUF Program 23 survey sites. The North American surveys show slightly higher proportions of any drug use (65 per cent compared with 61 per cent) and slightly lower proportions of multiple drug use (21 per cent compared with 27 per cent). The main difference between the English and American surveys in which the American percentages are higher is in relation to cocaine use which shows a percentage positive rate four times that of the English sites (40 per cent compared with 10 per cent).

The following two tables (Tables 3.2 and 3.3) breakdown the results of the urinalysis by sex, age, ethnic group, and suspected offence (an additional breakdown by location is shown in Appendix D).

The first table (Table 3.2) shows that for most drug types females were as, or more likely, to test positive as males. Females were significantly more likely than males (p>.05) to test positive for opiates and a higher percentage of females than males tested positive for methadone, cocaine, amphetamines, and benzodiazepines (although these differences were not statistically significant). Males were significantly more likely than females to test positive for cannabis and for alcohol (p<.001 and p<.05 respectively).

Males were statistically more likely than females to test positive for one or more drugs (p<.05). However, this relationship disappeared once alcohol was excluded from the calculation. Excluding both alcohol and cannabis from the calculation, results in females being significantly more likely than males to test positive for one or more drugs. There was no difference among males and females in the proportion who tested positive for multiple drugs. However, excluding alcohol and cannabis from the calculation shows that a higher percentage of females than males tested positive for multiple drugs (but the difference was not statistically significant).

Older arrestees (aged 21 or more) were more likely than younger arrestees (aged 16 to 20) to test positive for opiates (p<.001), methadone (p<.01), and cocaine (p<.05). However, younger detainees were more likely than older detainees to test positive for cannabis. Little is known about the association between age and use of opiates, methadone, and cocaine among the general population as the results of the main national and regional surveys tend not to identify a sufficiently large number of users to observe a trend. However, the current results suggest that, among the arrestee sub-population, younger people are less likely than older people to have recently consumed one of the 'hard' drugs.

There was no difference among the age groups in terms of testing positive for any drug. However, once alcohol was excluded the youngest group was more likely than the oldest group to test positive for any drug. Once alcohol and cannabis were excluded, the distribution reverts back to showing that the older group was more likely than the younger group to test positive for any drug. The different results are primarily a product of the fact that younger detainees were more likely to test positive for cannabis and older detainees were more likely to test positive for alcohol. Older arrestees were significantly more likely than younger arrestees to test positive for multiple drugs (p<.01). This effect remained even after excluding first alcohol and then alcohol and cannabis from the calculation.

Table 3.2: Percentage positive tests among arrestees by sex and age

	Sex		Age		
	Males	Females	16-20	21-30	31 or more
n=622[1]	548	71	191	258	158
Cannabis	49	25 ***	54	47	37 **
Opiates	17	28 *	11	26	17 ***
Methadone	7	13	2	11	10 **
Cocaine	10	14	5	14	10 *
Amphetamines	10	14	7	14	10
Benzodiazepines	12	13	8	15	14
Alcohol	26	16 *	24	19	38 ***
Multiple drugs					
[all drugs]	34	34	25	40	38 **
[excluding alcohol]	27	30	17	34	28 ***
[excluding alcohol and cannabis]	14	20	5	19	17 ***
Any drug					
[all drugs]	76	65 *	76	75	76
[excluding alcohol]	61	55	64	65	53 *
[excluding alcohol and cannabis]	33	47 *	25	42	36 ***

Notes: [1] Includes only those arrestees who provided a specimen (n=622). The 'n' for some variables does not always
add to the total 'n' as a result of missing information.
* p<.05; ** p<.01; ***p<.001 (Chi-squared test: corrected for 2X2 tables). Cells without any of the above symbols
were either 'not significant' (p>.05) or 'not applicable' (certain conditions of the Chi-squared test were not met).

The second table (Table 3.3) shows the relationship between ethnic group and urinalysis results. During the interview, respondents were invited to classify themselves into one of 12 ethnic groups (including an option of adding another group name of their choice not included in the list). As the number of respondents coded in each of the 12 categories was sometimes very small (and in most cases too small to conduct meaningful statistical analysis), respondents were aggregated for the purpose of analysis into just two groups (white and non-white). This method of analysis has the disadvantage of loss of information relating to individual ethnic groups. However, it has the advantage that it enables the possibility of detecting broad differences between the aggregated ethnic groups which otherwise would not have been possible.

White arrestees were significantly more likely than non-white arrestees to test positive for amphetamines (p<.01) and alcohol (p<.05) and were more likely to test positive for benzodiazepines, opiates, and methadone (although these associations were not statistically significant). Non-white arrestees were significantly more likely than white arrestees to test positive for cannabis (p<.05) and cocaine (p<.01). There was little difference among the two groups in terms of the proportion testing positive for any drug or for multiple drugs even after excluding alcohol and cannabis.

Table 3.3: Percentage positive tests among arrestees by ethnic group and suspected offence

	Ethnic group		Offence type			
	White	Non-white	Person	Property	Alcohol/drugs	Disorder
n=622[1]	519	68	85	306	54	53
Cannabis	44	59 *	46	50	45	32
Opiates	19	16	17	23	11	8
Methadone	8	6	4	11	0	4 *
Cocaine	9	21 **	5	14	7	2 *
Amphetamines	12	0 **	6	12	16	4
Benzodiazepines	13	6	12	16	7	8
Alcohol	28	13 *	24	20	52	54 ***
Multiple drugs						
[all drugs]	35	31	26	42	32	26
[excluding alcohol]	27	27	21	35	20	10 ***
[excluding alcohol and cannabis]	15	12	11	20	7	4 **
Any drug						
[all drugs]	75	72	72	76	96	76 **
[excluding alcohol]	60	66	59	67	63	44 *
[excluding alcohol and cannabis]	35	29	29	42	34	20 **

Notes: [1] Includes only those arrestees who provided a specimen (n=622). The 'n' for some variables does not always add to the total 'n' as a result of missing information.
* p<.05; ** p<.01; ***p<.001 (Chi-squared: corrected for 2X2 tables). Cells without any of the above symbols were either 'not significant' (p>.05) or 'not applicable' (certain conditions of the Chi-squared test were not met).

The offence for which the arrestee was currently held was recoded into four major groups: offences against the person, against property, alcohol and drug offences, and disorder offences. Detainees who did not provide a specimen, who were not held under suspicion of commission of an offence, or who were held for other offences were excluded from this part of the analysis. The following gives a breakdown of the distribution of cases.

•	property offenders	306
•	offenders against the person	85
•	alcohol/drug offenders	54
•	disorder offenders	53
	Total	**498**
•	other/not applicable	124
•	no specimen	217
	Total	**839**

23

Arrestees held for property offences were more likely than their counterparts to test positive for cocaine (p<.05), methadone (p<.01 and opiates (p<.05). Arrestees held for alcohol/drugs offences or for disorder offences were more likely than their counterparts to test positive for alcohol (p<.001). Arrestees held for alcohol or drugs offences were more likely to test positive for any drug (including alcohol) than arrestees held for other offences. Once alcohol was excluded from the calculation, the results show that arrestees held for property offences were more likely than arrestees held for other offences to test positive for any drug or for multiple drugs.

A summary of a breakdown of the percentage of positive tests by offence type in relation to property offences only is shown in Table 3.4. A more detailed breakdown of percentage positive tests for all offence types is included in Table D.5 in Appendix D.

Selected findings from Table 3.4 are listed below:

- Almost half (47%) of all arrestees held for shoplifting tested positive for opiates.

- Almost one-third (30%) of all arrestees held for shoplifting tested positive for cocaine.

- Almost one-quarter (23%) of all arrestees held for theft of a motor vehicle tested positive for opiates.

- Almost one-third (31%) of all arrestees held for theft of a motor vehicle tested positive for amphetamines.

- One in ten (11%) of arrestees held for burglary in a dwelling tested positive for opiates.

- Over one-quarter (26%) of arrestees held for burglary in a dwelling tested positive for alcohol.

- Over 80 percent of all arrestees held for theft of a motor vehicle, taking a vehicle without the owner's consent, shoplifting, and burglary in a dwelling tested positive for at least one drug.

Table 3.4: Percentage positive tests among arrestees by main offence type: property offences only

	Cannabis	Opiates	Meth-adone	Cocaine	Amphet-amines	Benzo-diazepines	Alcohol	% of arrestees with pos. test	Total offences (a) [1]	Total offences (b) [2]
Burglary (dwelling)	71	11	0	0	14	11	26	80	35	39
Burglary (non-dwelling)	52	28	8	4	20	24	16	76	25	29
Burglary (unspecified)	67	17	0	17	0	0	17	83	6	7
Robbery	58	5	0	5	11	11	32	68	19	25
Theft (person)	58	25	0	8	0	8	0	58	12	16
Theft (dwelling)	100	0	0	0	0	0	0	100	1	3
Theft (employee)	0	25	0	0	0	0	25	50	4	5
Theft (cycle)	60	0	0	20	0	0	0	60	5	7
Theft (from vehicle)	56	11	6	11	0	11	6	78	18	26
Theft (of vehicle)	42	23	12	15	31	12	19	81	26	30
Theft (TWOC)	73	9	0	9	18	27	36	91	11	15
Theft (shops)	43	47	29	30	8	20	12	80	90	128
Theft (machine)	67	0	0	0	0	0	0	67	3	3
Theft (other)	47	13	7	13	13	13	33	73	15	17
Handling	0	0	0	0	0	0	0	0	1	4
Fraud (deception)	45	5	0	5	18	9	0	45	22	30
Other offences not included in the table/missing	*	*	*	*	*	*	*	*	328	455
Total	*	*	*	*	*	*	*	*	621	839

Notes: The full version of this table is shown in Appendix D, Table D5.
[1] Total offences (a)=Offences relating only to those arrestees who provided a urine specimen.
[2] Total offences (b)=Offences relating to all arrestees interviewed.
All percentages are based on 'Total offences (a)'.

Overall, the results produced what might be regarded as surprising findings. Some offences not typically thought of as associated with drug misuse showed high levels of positive tests among arrestees. The finding that 23 per cent of arrestees held under suspicion of theft of a vehicle tested positive for opiates was much higher than average for the sample as a whole. The finding that 47 per cent of arrestees held for shoplifting tested positive for opiates and 30 per cent tested positive for cocaine was also higher than average (and perhaps surprising considering that shoplifting is not typically regarded as an important link in the drugs-crime connection).

Conversely, some offences more typically thought of as associated with drug use and drug-related crime showed relatively lower levels of positive tests among arrestees. The findings that five per cent of arrestees held for robbery tested positive for opiates and five per cent tested positive for cocaine were lower than the average rates for the sample as a whole. Similarly, the findings that 11 per cent of arrestees held for burglary in a dwelling tested positive for opiates and none tested positive for cocaine were lower than average prevalence rates.

Self-reports

All arrestees were interviewed prior to a request for a urine specimen and all arrestees were asked about their illegal drug use (defined as drugs that you are not supposed to take) in their lifetime, in the last 12 months, in the last month, and in the last three days. The respondents were asked about the use of 17 types of drugs which are commonly used illegally, plus a fictitious drug (semeron) and alcohol and tobacco. The results relating to drug use ever, over the last 12 months, and over the last month are shown below in Table 3.5. The results for lifetime prevalence of all arrestees and those aged 16-29 are compared with the results of the 1996 British Crime Survey relating to the general population aged 16-59 years and 16-29 respectively.

The table shows that over half of all arrestees reported using amphetamines, amyl nitrite, cannabis, and LSD at some point in their lifetimes. Over one-third of arrestees reported using cocaine, ecstasy, magic mushrooms, and temazepam. These percentage lifetime figures are substantially higher than those shown for the general population. The closest comparison is among the general population aged 16-29 and the arrestee sample aged 16-29. The ratios of the prevalence of general population use to arrestee use is shown in the final column in the table. The lifetime prevalence percentage ratio for arrestees compared with the general population was one in 27 for heroin and one in 26 for crack. In addition, the arrestee percentage was over five times the general population percentage in relation to cocaine, ecstasy, solvents, and LSD. The arrestee population was twice as likely to report using cannabis than the general population.

The prevalence figures for the last month show that over half of arrestees reported using cannabis in the last month and one-quarter admitted using amphetamines in the last month. Almost one in ten arrestees said that they had used cocaine in the last month and the same proportion said that they had used crack. One in six arrestees said that they had used heroin in the last month.

These percentages (notably those for heroin, cocaine, and crack) are about the same or slightly lower than the percentage of arrestees testing positive for these drugs. One reasons for the difference in results is possible under-reporting of drug use during the interviews. The extent and effect of under-reporting and over-reporting is discussed in more detail in Appendix B.

Table 3.5: *Percentage of arrestees reporting using particular drugs ever, in the last year and in the last month and percentage of the general population using particular drugs in the last month*

n=839	Arrestees				1996 British Crime Survey (Ramsay and Spiller, 1997)			
	Percentage using ever		Percentage using in last year	Percentage using in last month	Percentage using ever [1]		Ratio of general population to arrestee	
	All	Aged 16-29	All	All	All	Aged 16-29	All	Aged 16-29
Amphetamines	65	70	44	25	9	16	1:7	1:4
Amyl nitrite	52	58	19	6	6	14	1:9	1:4
Barbiturates	11	10	5	2	*	*	*	*
Cannabis	82	87	70	59	22	36	1:4	1:2
Cocaine	36	34	20	9	3	4	1:12	1:9
Crack	25	26	17	9	1	1	1:25	1:26
DF118s	19	19	13	6	*	*	*	*
Diazepam	28	28	19	11	*	*	*	*
Diconal	7	6	3	1	*	*	*	*
Ecstasy	45	53	29	13	3	9	1:15	1:6
Solvents	31	38	4	1	2	5	1:16	1:8
Heroin	27	27	21	16	1	1	1:27	1:27
LSD	55	63	20	6	5	10	1:11	1:6
Magic mushrooms	38	39	9	1	5	9	1:8	1:4
Methadone	21	20	16	10	0 [2]	0 [2]	*	*
Temazepam	43	46	26	13	*	*	*	*
Temgesic	15	17	8	2	*	*	*	*
Alcohol	98	97	91	83	*	*	*	*
Tobacco	90	90	84	83	*	*	*	*
Multiple drugs [3]	78	82	62	44	*	*	*	*
Any drug [3]	88	91	77	67	*	*	*	*

Notes: [1] BCS, 1996, core sample; all= ages 16-59.
       [2] Less than 0.5%.
       [3] Including alcohol and tobacco.

Conclusion

The current chapter has shown that a high proportion of all arrestees tested positive for illegal drugs at the time of arrest and a high proportion of them admitted to drug use. The prevalence figures shown are higher than those recorded among the general population and higher in some instances than those recorded in other arrestee and prison populations. The results show that females are generally just as likely to test positive for illegal drugs as males. White arrestees are more likely than non-white arrestees to test positive for amphetamines and alcohol, while non-white arrestees are more likely than white arrestees to test positive for cannabis and cocaine.

4 Drugs and crime

Introduction

The publications resulting from the DUF Program in the United States tend to be fairly cautious about what the results from drug testing and interviewing arrestees can tell us about the links between drug use and crime. One argument found in the literature is that it cannot be determined from urinalysis results whether drugs were used before or after the crime was committed (Wish and Gropper, 1990). However, there are other connections between drug use and crime that can be determined from drug testing and interviewing arrestees.

The question of the connection between drugs use and crime is investigated in the current chapter in terms of the extent to which drug use is associated with higher levels of criminal behaviour than non-drug use. The results of the current research can be brought to bear on this issue in four main ways: (1) determining the proportion of arrestees who use various kinds of drugs; (2) determining arrestees perceptions of the connection between their drug use and criminal behaviour; (3) determining the correlation between measures of crime and measures of drug use; and (4) estimating the contribution of drug use to crime in terms of numbers of additional crimes committed and amounts of additional illegal income generated.

The proportion of arrestees who are drugs users

A large part of early research on the links between drugs and crime comprised an attempt to establish the proportion of drug users among samples of criminals (usually the proportion of addicts or drug users among prison populations) or the proportion of criminals among drug users (usually the proportion of individuals who have been convicted of a criminal offence among in-patient or out-patient treatment groups) (Bennett, 1991). There are a number of problems with research based on prison populations and treatment populations. The populations tend to include only the most chronic cases of criminals or drug users and information about drugs and crime tends to be collected a long time after the criminal events. The establishment of the DUF Program in the United States based on interviews and urine collection among arrestees substantially improved the quality of this kind of research. Arrestees encompass a much wider range of potential criminals and information is collected about them at a point much closer to the time of the criminal event. Until the current research, there was no similar programme in Britain and little was known about the proportion of arrestees who were drug users (with the exception of research by Robertson et al. [1995] and Chatterton et al. [1995] mentioned earlier).

The results of the current research on the prevalence of drug use among arrestees have been presented in the preceding chapter. The research has shown that the majority of arrestees tested positive for one or more drugs and a substantial minority of detainees tested positive for the addictive and expensive-to-finance drugs (such as heroin and cocaine). However, in order to show a link between drug use and crime it would have to be shown (using prevalence rates as a method of analysis) that the prevalence rates among arrestees was higher than expected. Specifically, it would have to be shown that these rates were higher than a comparable non-criminal or less criminal sample.

The research was not designed to make comparisons between criminal and non-criminal samples. However, some limited comparison can be made with the results of research based on the general population. The results presented in the previous chapter showed that the arrestee samples were much more likely than the general population samples to use drugs (Ramsay and Spiller, 1997). In particular, arrestees were more likely than the general population to report using those drugs types which are believed to be associated with crime. However, the arrestee samples and the general population samples generated as part of the British Crime Survey are not identical in terms of other characteristics.

The most effective comparison that could be made using this method of analysis is to compare a criminal population with a non-criminal population which in all other ways is identical or nearly identical to it. However, there is no sample of non-criminal, non-arrestees identical to the sample of arrestees which could be used to make such a comparison. Until such a comparison can be made, the evidence from the current research relating to the high prevalence rates among arrestees can only be taken as suggestive of a link between drug use and criminal behaviour. However, the evidence from this one method of analysis can be combined with other pieces of evidence derived from the other methods of analysis discussed below.

Perceptions of the connection between drugs and crime

The second piece of evidence concerns arrestees' reports about whether they thought that their drug use and their offending were connected. All arrestees who reported that they used at least one drug type over the last 12 months were asked whether they thought that their drug use and crime were connected. A similar question was asked about the connection between their drinking and crime. The results are shown in Tables 4.1 and 4.2 below.

Table 4.1: Perceived connection between drug use and crime by location
Percentages

Is your drug use connected to your offending? [1]	Sunder- land n=181	Notting- ham n=170	Cam- bridge n=128	London n=78	Man- chester n=91	Total n=648
Yes	36	40	55	57	50	46
(Drugs lead to crime)						
Effect of drugs on judgement	13	8	21	16	12	13
Need for money to buy drugs	12	20	19	17	30	19
(Crime leads to drugs)						
Money from crime buys drugs	3	1	4	1	1	2
(Other connections)						
A combination of the above	5	4	9	10	7	6
Other connections	3	7	2	13	0	5
No	64	60	45	43	50	54
Total	100	100	100	100	100	100

Notes: [1] Includes drugs users in the last 12 months only (excluding alcohol and tobacco).

Table 4.2: Perceived connection between alcohol use and crime by location
Percentages

Is your alcohol use connected to your offending? [1]	Sunder-land n=257	Notting-ham n=185	Cam-bridge n=137	London n=87	Man-chester n=93	Total n=759
Yes	46	37	33	37	37	39
(Alcohol leads to crime)						
Affect of alcohol on judgement	38	28	25	32	32	32
Need for money to buy alcohol	1	2	5	1	2	2
(Crime leads to alcohol)						
Money from crime buys alcohol	0	1	0	0	0	*
(Other connections)						
A combination of the above	3	4	3	2	1	3
Other connections	4	2	0	2	2	3
No	54	63	67	63	63	61
Total	100	100	100	100	100	100

Notes: [1] Includes alcohol users in the last 12 months only.

The proportion of arrestees who used at least one drug in the last 12 months who thought that their drug use and criminal behaviour were connected ranged from one-third (36%) in Sunderland to over one-half (57%) in London. The majority of arrestees who thought that their drug use and criminal behaviour were connected gave reasons which fell into the 'drug-use-causes-crime' category and relatively few arrestees gave reasons that fell in the 'crime-leads-to-drug-use' category. The two most frequent connections given were that drug use affected judgement in some way or that crimes were committed in order to finance drug use.

Somewhat similar results were obtained in relation to alcohol use and crime. The proportion of arrestees who thought that their alcohol use and criminal behaviour were connected ranged from about one-third (33%) in Cambridge to almost half (46%) in Sunderland. The majority of arrestees who thought that their alcohol use and criminal behaviour were connected gave reasons which fell into the category of 'alcohol-use-causes-crime' category and relatively few arrestees gave reasons that fell in the 'crime-leads-to-alcohol-use' category. Very few arrestees gave reasons that related to the need for money to buy alcohol or the use of money from crime to buy alcohol. The most frequent connection given was that alcohol use affected judgement in some way.

Hence, the findings indicate that drugs and offending are believed to be linked by some arrestees, but not by others. It is possible that some arrestees will over-estimate the link, while others will under-estimate the link and that some of the variation among arrestees may be due to reporting variations. However, it is also possible that the general balance of responses is more or less correct and that drug use and crime are connected for some arrestees, but not for others.

It would be expected (if drug use served to increase the rate of offending among some offenders) that arrestees who said that there was a link between their drug use and criminal behaviour would commit more (or different) crimes than those who did not. It would also be expected that arrestees who said that there was a link between their drug use and criminal behaviour would consume more (or different) drugs than those who did not.

The following table (Table 4.3) shows the relationship between mean illegal income and mean expenditure on drugs during the last 12 months and whether or not arrestees believed that their drug use and criminal behaviour were connected. Mean illegal income was calculated from a question which asked arrestees to state their total income over the last 12 months from all illegal sources. The question immediately followed a similarly phrased question which asked them to state their total income from all legal sources over the last 12 months (including wages and social security benefits). Their responses were coded either as a range (in which case the mid-point of the range was used in all calculations) or as a specific amount (in which case the specific amount was used in all calculations).

Arrestees who thought that their drug use and crime over the last 12 months were connected reported significantly higher levels of mean illegal income than those who did not. On average, arrestees who said that their drug use and crime were connected reported two to three times the amount of illegal income in the last year than those who did not. Similar variations were shown in relation to estimated expenditure on drugs. Detainees who stated that their drug use and crime were connected estimated between five to ten times the amount of expenditure on drugs over the last year as those who did not. Hence, arrestees who reported a connection between drug use and offending were much more involved in illegal income generating crime and also much more involved in expensive drug consumption than their counterparts.

Table 4.3: Perceived connection between drug use and crime by estimated mean illegal income and estimated expenditure on drugs in the last 12 months

Percentages

Drug users in last 12 months only	Sunder- land n=181	Notting- ham n=170	Cam- bridge n=128	London n=78	Man- chester n=91
Mean illegal income (£s)					
No connection	3,291	4,348	4,095	3,172	5,721
Connection	10,484	13,887	8,661	7,808	12,894
Mean expenditure on drugs (£s)					
No connection	1,022	1,048	2,388	971	2,475
Connection	5,784	10,061	7,089	5,591	13,199

Notes: All differences of means are statistically significant at p<.05.

Figure 4.1 provides additional information on the relationship between perceived connection between drugs and crime and use of drugs. The results of the urinalysis were used to examine in more detail the relationship between the perceived drugs-crime connection and the percentage of arrestees who tested positive for various drugs. The figure shows that (on average) the greater the number of positive tests the greater the percentage of arrestees who believed that their drug use and crime were connected. Hence, the number of positive drug tests provides some estimation of the proportion of arrestees who believe that their drug use and crime are connected.

The preceding analysis suggests that drug use and crime might be connected in relation to some offenders, but might not be connected in relation to others. Arrestees who believed that their drug use and crime were connected were more heavily involved in drug use and criminal behaviour than those who did not believe that their drug use and crime were connected.

Correlation of measures of drug use and measures of criminality

One way of determining a link between drug use and criminal behaviour is to examine the correlation between measures of drug use and measures of criminality. The main measures of drug use used in the current research were: (1) urinalysis results, (2) self-reported expenditure on drugs, and (3) self-reported drug use. The main measures of criminal behaviour used in the current research were: (1) estimated illegal income, and (2) (in the last survey only) self-reported criminal behaviour. The following analysis

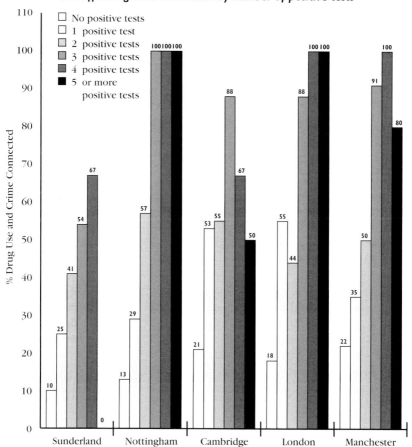

Figure 4.1 Percentage of respondents who thought that their drug use and offending were connected by number of positive tests

examines the correlation between these various measures of drugs and criminality.

Urinalysis results and illegal income

The following table (Table 4.4) shows the relationship between the urinalysis results (as a measure of drug use) and illegal income (as a measure of crime). One of the hypotheses being tested in this analysis is that arrestees who test positive for drugs that are known to be expensive to finance will be more heavily involved in illegal income generation than those who do not test positive for these drugs.

The table shows that overall arrestees who tested positive for one or more drug types tended to report higher levels of illegal income than those who tested positive for no drugs. Overall, arrestees who tested negative for drugs (including alcohol) reported an average of just over £3,000 illegal income in the last 12 months compared with an average of almost £11,000 for those who tested positive for four drug types. Similar differences in illegal income can be observed when excluding alcohol from the number of drug types. The correlation between number of positive tests and estimated illegal income was statistically significant (p<.001) in relation to both methods of analysis (i.e. including and excluding alcohol).

The results also show that the differences between positive and negative test results and the amount of illegal income reported are much greater in relation to those drug types most commonly identified as being linked with crime (opiates, methadone, and cocaine). Arrestees testing positive for opiates reported almost three times the amount of illegal income as those who tested negative and almost four times the amount as those who tested negative for all drugs (p<.001). Similar differences were shown in relation to methadone with arrestees who tested positive for this drug estimating two to three times the amount of illegal income compared with those who tested negative. Arrestees who tested positive for cocaine also reported at least twice the amount of illegal income as those who tested negative (the very high levels of income shown for Sunderland may have been the effect of the small number of cases involved).

Arrestees who tested positive for cannabis, amphetamines or benzodiazepines were no more likely than their counterparts to report high levels of illegal income. Arrestees who tested positive for alcohol were significantly less likely than those who did not to report high levels of illegal income. Overall, testing positive for alcohol was associated with only a small (and non-significant) increase in illegal income, compared with testing negative for all drugs. One reason why arrestees testing positive for alcohol reported lower levels of illegal income concerns the nature of the offences for which they were currently held. Table D.5. in Appendix D shows that high proportions of positive tests for alcohol were often found in relation to drink-related offences, offences against the person, and disorder offences, which, by their nature, do not generate income.

In general, the results of this section are consistent with the hypothesis that certain kinds of drug use are associated with the commission of income-generating crime.

Table 4.4: Urinalysis results by mean illegal income over the last 12 months by location

	Sunder-land n=209	Notting-ham n=132	Cam-bridge n=124[1]	London n=79[1]	Man-chester n=77[1]	All n=621
Cannabis						
Positive	4,406	8,738	7391	5,171	8,449	6,569
Negative	5,044	6,935	5,477	2,806	9,477	5,587
Opiates						
Positive	15,027 ***	16,525 **	10,800 *	5,000	13,990 **	12,674 ***
Negative	3,284	4,876	5,467	3,820	6,377	4,394
Methadone						
Positive	39,000 ***	13,800	5,417	3,719	14,309 **	12,167 ***
Negative	4,313 [2]	7,179	6,630	4,105	7,318	5,529
Cocaine						
Positive	45,000 ***	9,958	7,813	5,024	13,976 **	11,225 ***
Negative	4,224 [2]	7,381	6,500	3,705	6,936	5,417
Amphetamines						
Positive	2,367	5,156	11,750 **	2,625	14,357	7,720
Negative	5,049	8,098	5,540	4,103	8,326	5,868
Benzodiazepines						
Positive	10,536 *	11,950	6,827	3,273	8,329	8,312
Negative	4,136	7,366	6,509	4,197	9,066	5,716
Alcohol						
Positive	3,427	3,992	8,365	3,735	4,667	4,046
Negative	5,822	8,646	6,329	4,158	9,243	6,699
Number of positive tests [3]						
0	2,617	2,448	2,929 *	2,179	6,550	3,065 ***
1	4,193	8,168	6,528	4,305	6,148	5,482
2	6,783	11,027	8,669	4,103	11,167	7,775
3	8,057	9,870	15,625	6,679	11,318	10,187
4	19,167	10,600	6,667	4,458	13,806	10,827
5	-	13,000	625	-	12,300	8,583
Number of positive tests [4]						
0	3,226 ***	2,861	3,469 *	2,429	5,779	3,351 ***
1	3,844	9,737	6,489	4,095	7,058	5,763
2	9,808	11,319	9,850	5,889	8,500	9,117
3	11,189	12,088	14,286	4,250	14,250	12,123
4	50,000	10,600	6,667	4,600	13,806	11,750
5	-	13,000	625	1,500	12,300	8,583

Notes: [1] In Cambridge, London, and Manchester (the first three surveys), arrestees were asked to state in which range of preset income groups their illegal income fell (whereas in the other surveys arrestees were asked to provide a single-figure estimate of their illegal income). In order to provide comparable responses, the actual illegal income over the last year for arrestees in Cambridge was estimated for each arrestee as the mid-point of the income range chosen.

[2] The number of arrestees testing positive for this drug was low (n=3) which may have distorted the average.

[3] Including alcohol.

[4] Excluding alcohol.

* p<.05; ** p<.01; ***p<.001. (Significance test=Analysis of Variance.)

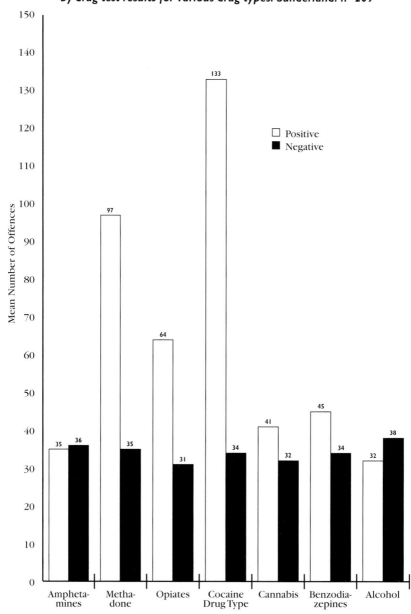

Figure 4.2 Mean number of offences committed in the last 12 months by drug test results for various drug types: Sunderland: n=209

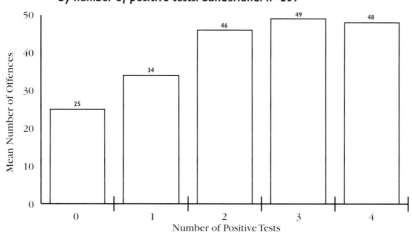

Figure 4.3 Mean number of offences committed in the last 12 months by number of positive tests: Sunderland: n=209

Urinalysis results and self-reported offending

In the previous section, illegal income was used as a measure of criminal involvement. In the final survey, in Sunderland, an additional measure of criminal involvement was added to the questionnaire concerning arrestees' self-reported offending. Arrestees were asked whether they had committed each of 10 property offences in the last 12 months and (if so) they were asked how many times they had committed the offence. The selected offences were chosen from the most likely income-generating offences associated with drug use, namely: theft of a motor vehicle, theft from a motor vehicle, shoplifting, burglary dwelling, burglary non-dwelling, robbery, theft person, fraud/deception, handling stolen goods, and drugs supply.

Figures 4.2 and 4.3 show the mean number of offences committed in relation to drug test results for various drug types and in relation to the number of positive tests. The total number of offences reported was recorded as the addition of all reported offences across the 10 offence types. However, arrestees who reported over 200 offences in the last year were coded as committing 200 offences. This was done in order to smooth out the distribution in order to avoid unusual effects due to the small number of very high-rate offenders. The mean value of the raw scores before applying a cut-off at 200 offences was 88 offences in the last 12 months (ranging from 0 to 2,800) and the mean value after applying a cut-off at 200 was 33 offences in the last 12 months (ranging from 0 to 200). It is unknown to what extent these figures are generalisable to other locations.

Figure 4.2 shows that arrestees who test positive for opiates, methadone, and cocaine report a greater number of offences than their counterparts. It also shows that arrestees testing positive for amphetamines or alcohol tend not to report higher rates of offending than those who test negative (instead they show slightly lower rates). (It should be noted that the sample sizes were small in relation to methadone and cocaine and some caution should be taken in interpreting the extent of the variation in relation to these drugs.) Overall, these findings are very much in line with the previous analysis which was based on illegal income as a measure of crime.

Figure 4.3 also supports the earlier finding and shows a fairly linear positive relationship between mean number of offences committed and number of positive drug tests. Arrestees who tested positive for two or more drug types reported almost twice as many offences as those who tested negative for all drugs. As was found in the previous analysis, the measure of criminal behaviour increased to a plateau at about three or four positive tests and remained stable or declined with additional positive tests.

Expenditure on drugs and illegal income

In the present section the relationship between drug use and crime is examined by looking at estimated expenditure on drugs as a measure of drug use and illegal income as a measure of crime. Table 4.5 shows that the two variables are strongly correlated. All calculations in this section are based on the amount spent on drugs excluding alcohol and tobacco.

Overall (and in relation to each location) the amount of illegal income increases as the amount spent on drugs increases. Arrestees who reported spending less than £2,000 on drugs in the last 12 months reported on average just over £3,000 worth of illegal income. Arrestees who reported spending £10,000 or more on drugs in the last 12 months reported on average just over £19,000 worth of illegal income. The correlation between expenditure on drugs and illegal income was r=.52 and was statistically significant (Pearson's correlation coefficient: p<.001).

Expenditure on drugs and self-reported crime

The following chart (Figure 4.4) shows the relationship between expenditure on drugs and self-reported crime in relation to arrestees in Sunderland. The chart shows a gradual increase in mean number of offences committed as the annual expenditure on drugs increases. The relationship between the two variables was statistically significant (p<.001).

Table 4.5: Amount spent on drugs over the last 12 months by mean illegal income over the last 12 months by location

	Sunder-land n=271	Notting-ham n=209	Cam-bridge n=152	London n=103	Man-chester n=104	All n=839
Amount spent on drugs						
£Nil	1,128	3,057	3,261	1,811	4,565	2,209
£1–£1,999	3,321	3,406	3,594	1,191	4,038	3,252
£2,000–£4,999	7,969	3,779	6,959	9,990	5,706	7,128
£5,000–£9,999	16,999	10,770	7,321	11,321	14,406	11,703
£10,000 or more	22,750	25,184	18,929	10,056	16,519	19,020
Significance	***	***	***	***	***	***
Area mean for all groups	3,994	8,030	6,224	5,206	8,803	5,899

Notes: *p<.05; **p<.01; ***p<.001. (Significance test=Analysis of Variance)
Mean illegal income and amount spent are expressed as £'s.

Figure 4.4 Mean number of offences committed in the last 12 months by mean expenditure on drugs in the last 12 months: Sunderland: n=271

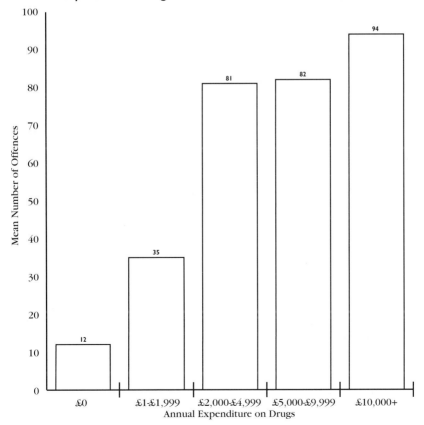

Self-reported drug use and illegal income

A third measure of drug use was created for the purpose of analysis based on arrestees' admissions of drug use within the last 12 months in relation to 17 categories of drug (excluding alcohol and tobacco). The following chart compares this measure of drug use with mean levels of estimated illegal income.

The chart shows a linear and positive relationship between number of drug types used in the last 12 months and estimated illegal income over the same period. Hence, the more drug types used (i.e. the more the user moves towards poly-drug use) the greater the level of illegal income generated.

Figure 4.5 *Mean illegal income in the last 12 months by number of drug types used in the last 12 months: All areas: n=839*

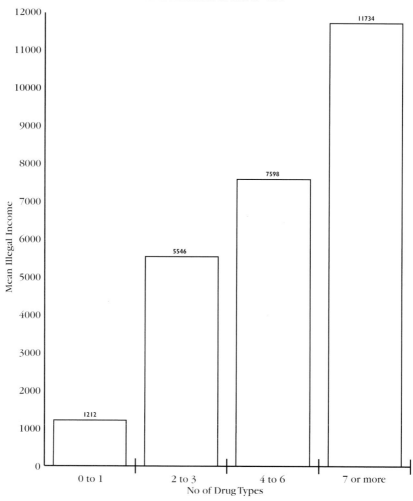

Self-reported drug use and self-reported crime

The final chart in this section shows the relationship between self-reported drug use and self-reported crime. The chart shows a strong positive correlation between number of drug types used in the last 12 months and mean number of offences committed. Arrestees who reported using seven or more drug types reported 10 times the mean number of offences of arrestees who reported using no drugs or just one drug (bearing in mind that the maximum number of offences reported was kept at a ceiling of 200 per arrestee).

Figure 4.6 Mean number of offences committed in the last 12 months by mean number of drug types in the last 12 months: Sunderland: n=271

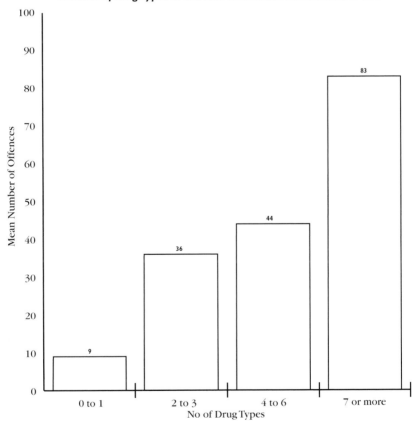

Explaining the contribution of drug use to crime

The preceding analysis has shown that various measures of drug use and various measures of crime were significantly correlated. These results indicate that levels of drug use and levels of criminal involvement are closely associated. Arrestees who are heavily involved in drug use were also heavily involved in criminal behaviour. The results also indicate that certain kinds of drug use (namely use of opiates, methadone, and cocaine) tend to be more closely associated with criminal involvement than other kinds of drug use.

However, the results as they stand do not tell us the extent to which drug use causes crime. In order to estimate causality, it would be necessary to establish not only the existence of a correlation between drug use and crime, but also the temporal direction of the two variables and the extent to which other variables partly or wholly explain the correlation. The research was not designed to answer questions about temporal order or about the impact of other variables which might independently explain both drug use and crime. However, the research has collected some data which bears on these issues and some limited analysis can be conducted.

One method of determining causality between drug use and crime, is to generate a causal model whereby a number of the independent variables (possible causal variables including drug use) are entered into a formula which attempts to explain criminal behaviour (in this case, frequency or rate of offending). Ideally, the model should include temporal variables (e.g. drug use at various periods of time) and other rival explanatory variables (variables which might independently explain drug use or crime). The research has not collected sufficient data for a thorough analysis of this kind. However, it is possible to devise a simplified model from the data which have been collected.

The method adopted to achieve this was to use multivariate analysis of variance in an attempt to estimate criminal involvement from a list of independent variables. The main measure of criminal involvement used is self-reported illegal income over the last 12 months. Various individual, social, and economic explanatory variables and drug use variables were entered into a linear equation in order to explain variations in illegal income. The measures of drug use were limited to self-reported heroin, methadone, cocaine and crack use within the last three days. This measure has an advantage over the use of the urinalysis results as it distinguishes between crack and cocaine. It also has an advantage over the use of self-reports over a lifetime, or the last year, or the last month in that it is most likely to capture frequent users.

The results of the analysis are shown in Tables 4.6 and 4.7 below. The first table shows that none of the individual, social, or economic factors entered into the equation explained a significant proportion of the variation in illegal income. It also shows that neither methadone use nor cocaine use alone were significant in explaining criminal involvement once the effects of the other variables had been taken into account. The main explanatory variables were heroin use and crack use which were each significant after taking into account the effect of each other. Table 4.7 shows the adjusted mean values of illegal income associated with the presence or absence of these two variables in combination. The greatest illegal income (over £20,000 per year on average) is associated with use of both drugs. When used alone (without the other drug) the adjusted means drop to £13,000 for heroin and £10,000 for crack. When neither of the drugs is reported, the mean illegal income reduces to £3,000.

The effect of using only a limited number of explanatory variables has resulted in a model with fairly low predictive power (R-squared=.17). However, the exercise has served a useful purpose of identifying the independent effects of specific drug use variables in explaining criminal behaviour. The analysis shows that heroin or crack use over the last three days independently explains a significant part of the variance of illegal income, whereas methadone use and cocaine use over the last three days do not.

Table 4.6: The contribution of individual, social, economic and drug use variables in explaining illegal income using multivariate analysis of variance

n=839	F	Significance of F
Variables not in the equation		
Sex	2.7	ns
Age	*[1]	ns
Race	0.5	ns
Marital status	1.2	ns
Tenure	3.2	ns
Legal income	0.5	ns
Employment status	2.4	ns
Methadone use (alone)	2.8	ns
Cocaine use (alone)	0.1	ns
Variables in the equation		
Heroin use (alone)	58.1	p<.001
Crack use (alone)	13.8	p<.001
R-squared		0.17
Adjusted R-squared		0.17

Notes: [1] Entered as a covariate

Table 4.7: The contribution of various drug combinations to illegal income using multivariate analysis of variance

	Adjusted mean illegal income
Heroin use + crack use	20,284
Heroin use only	13,469
Crack use only	10,697
Neither heroin nor crack use	3,882

It is possible to take these estimations of the effect of drug use on crime one stage further. On the basis of the estimates of mean illegal income associated with various combinations of heroin and crack use shown in Table 4.7 above, it is possible to estimate what the total illegal income (and hence criminal involvement) of the sample of arrestees would have been had the heroin-crack and crime connection not existed. It is not necessary to prove causality to conduct this analysis as it is hypothetical (a 'what if' calculation).

The results of the analysis are shown in the following table (Table 4.8). The table shows the number of cases in the total sample which fall into the four categories investigated and the mean and total illegal income generated by these groups. The table also shows the revised mean and total illegal income for these groups had the level of illegal income been reduced to that shown for arrestees who used neither heroin nor crack. This shows that the total existing illegal income earned over the last 12 months by the 738 arrestees who were included in this analysis was £4,188,040. When the illegal incomes of arrestees using heroin and crack are reduced to the level of other arrestees, the total revised illegal income earned over the last 12 months reduces to £2,864,916 (a reduction of 32 per cent). Hence, the above estimation would suggest (bearing in mind all of the previous qualifications) that if drug use caused all of the higher levels of illegal income, then the absence of use of these drugs would reduce the criminal activity of the sample as a whole by one-third (bearing in mind that these five areas may not be representative of the country as a whole).

Table 4.8: Estimates of the effect of reducing mean illegal income among arrestees who reported using heroin or crack in the last three days to the mean illegal income of arrestees who did not report using these drugs

	No. of cases in the total sample	Existing mean illegal income	Existing total illegal income	Revised mean illegal income	Revised total illegal income	Percentage reduction from existing to revised total illegal income
Heroin use+crack use	39	20,284	791,076	3,882	151,398	80%
Heroin use-no crack	64	13,469	863,744	3,882	248,448	71%
Crack use-no heroin	10	10,697	106,970	3,882	38,820	64%
Neither heroin nor crack use	625	3,882	2,426,250	3,882	2,426,250	0%
Total	738		4,188,040		2,864,916	32%

Conclusion

The main aim of the current research was to estimate the prevalence of drug use among arrestees and the main methods used to do this were drug testing and interviewing. It was not an aim of the research to prove the existence of a causal connection between drug use and crime. Nevertheless, the data collected provided some insights into the nature of the connection which have not previously been identified among arrestees in Britain. The research has shown that a large proportion of arrestees are involved in drug use and many of these use addictive and expensive drugs. It has shown that a number of measures of drug use and crime are strongly correlated. A substantial proportion of arrestees (approximately half) believe that their drug use and crime are related. Finally, the research has shown that (on the basis of the findings from these five areas) use of heroin and crack cocaine may be responsible for inflating criminal involvement by as much as one-third.

5 Injecting drugs

Introduction

The issue of injecting drugs is important not only in relation to the health of the individual arrestee, but also in relation to the potential spread of disease within the population, including the HIV virus. All arrestees who reported that they had consumed at least one drug type in their lifetime were asked if they had ever injected one of four drugs (heroin, methadone, cocaine, and amphetamines), plus any additional drugs, ever, in the last 12 months, in the last month, and in the last three days.

Prevalence of injecting drugs

The results of the interview responses in relation to injecting ever and in the last 12 months are summarised in Table 5.1 below.

Table 5.1 Percentage of arrestees who reported injecting selected drugs in their lifetime and during the last 12 months

	Sunder-land n=271	Notting-ham n=209	Cam-bridge n=152	London n=103	Man-chester n=104	All n=839
Heroin						
Ever	6	13	18	16	22	13
Last 12 months	4	8	15	12	21	10
Methadone						
Ever	2	4	7	1	6	4
Last 12 months	1	3	3	0	6	2
Cocaine						
Ever	3	8	12	10	14	8
Last 12 months	1	4	7	6	14	5
Amphetamines						
Ever	10	17	25	15	19	16
Last 12 months	6	12	15	1	12	9
Any Drug Above						
Ever	11	21	28	16	25	19
Last 12 months	7	14	22	12	22	14

The results show that 19 per cent (1 in 5) of all arrestees admitted injecting at least one illegal drug at some time in their lives. Fourteen per cent of arrestees reported injecting drugs in the last 12 months. The results vary slightly by type of drug. Thirteen per cent of arrestees said that they had injected heroin in their lifetime and one in 10 of all arrestees said that they had injected heroin in the last 12 months. Approximately one in 10 arrestees said that had injected amphetamines in the last 12 months and one in 20 arrestees said that they had injected cocaine. Far fewer arrestees said that they had injected methadone. The results also vary slightly across the five study areas. The highest lifetime prevalence rates for injecting were found in Cambridge and Manchester with one-quarter of all arrestees stating that they had injected illegal drugs in their lifetime and one-fifth stating that they had done so in the last 12 months.

The lifetime prevalence rates for arrestees are generally higher than the same prevalence rates found among surveys of the general population. The following table compares the current research findings and other survey findings in terms of rates of injection. The table shows that the lifetime prevalence rate among the arrestees in the current research are up to 10 times higher than the rates shown for the three general population surveys (two local and one national).

Closer comparisons can be made in relation to the current research and other surveys of criminal populations. The table shows that higher rates of injection (28 per cent of the sample) were found in the survey of prisoners by Power et al. (1992). However, the closest comparison that can be made is with other surveys of arrestees. The only recent survey of this kind available is the DUF survey results for 1995. The injection rates are not published in the annual reports. However, they can be calculated directly from the DUF data which are available from the National Institute of Justice. The data show that a slightly lower percentage of arrestees (16%) from the 23 DUF sites reported ever injecting illegal drugs compared with the prevalence figures for the current research (19%). Arrestees in England were more likely than those in the United States to report injecting heroin and amphetamines, but were less likely to report injecting cocaine.

Table 5.2 Percentage of the total sample who had ever injected selected drugs across surveys

	General pop-ulation	General pop-ulation	General pop-ulation	Prisoners	Arrestees	Arrestees
	Leitner et al. (1993) [1]	Frischer et al. (1992) [2]	Ramsay and Spiller (1997) [3]	Power et al. (1992) [4]	DUF (1995) [5]	Five survey areas [6]
Heroin	*	*	*	*	11	13
Methadone	*	*	*	*	*	4
Cocaine	*	*	*	*	11	8
Amphetamines	*	*	*	*	6	16
Any drug	1-3	1-2	<1	28	16	19

Notes: [1] Main sample percentages across four areas;
[2] General population survey of Glasgow;
[3] This question was asked to respondents aged 16-59 who admitted drug use in the last 12 months and covered the period of the last 12 months (and not lifetime as shown for the other results);
[4] Cross-sectional sample from eight Scottish prisons;
[5] Calculated directly from the DUF data for 1995 (Part and Part II) and includes adult males and females;
[6] The percentage of all arrestees who reported injecting one or more of the four drug types shown.

Prevalence of needle sharing

One of the greatest areas of concern in relation to the injecting behaviour of arrestees is their involvement in sharing needles. During the processes of needle sharing, it is possible to transfer blood from one user to another, along with any related infections or diseases. All arrestees who admitted injecting at least one drug in their lifetime were asked if they had ever shared their syringes or needles. The results are shown in Table 5.3 below.

Table 5.3 Percentage of arrestees who reported sharing needles in their lifetime and during the last 12 months

	Sunder-land n=271	Notting-ham n=209	Cam-bridge n=152	London n=103	Man-chester n=104	All n=839
Shared ever						
n injected ever	30	43	43	16	26	158
% of whole sample	1	6	11	8	10	6
% of injectors ever	7	28	40	50	38	32
Shared in last 12 months						
n injected in last 12 months	20	30	33	12	23	118
% of whole sample	<1	3	7	3	4	3
% of injectors in the last 12 months	5	23	33	25	17	22

The table shows that six per cent of all arrestees had at some time in their life shared a needle. Almost one-third of arrestees who had ever injected illegal drugs had shared a needle at some time in their lives. The table also shows the percentage of arrestees sharing needles over the last 12 months. Three per cent of the total sample said that they had shared needles in this period and 22 per cent of all arrestees who injected over the last 12 months said that they had shared needles.

These figures are worrying for a number of reasons. The fact that about one in 17 of all arrestees passing through police custody suites within the research areas had shared a needle at some point in their lives and one in 33 had shared needles in the last 12 months is of some concern. It means that the police are regularly dealing with a high health risk population (on average about eight or nine arrestees a week had shared needles at some point in their lives and four or five arrestees a week had shared within the last 12 months).

Arrestees who had reported that they had injected at least one illegal drug in their lifetime were also asked why they shared (if they did) and why they did not share (if they did not). The responses are summarised in Table 5.4 below.

Table 5.4 Percentage of arrestees who reported specific reasons for sharing and not sharing

	Sunder-land n=271	Notting-ham n=209	Cam-bridge n=152	London n=103	Man-chester n=104
Reasons for sharing					
n injected and shared ever	*2*	*12*	*17*	*8*	*10*
Absence of clean needles	50	67	88	25	80
Convenient to share	0	0	0	38	0
No health risks/with friends only /with partner only	0	17	0	13	10
Didn't think about the consequences	50	17	12	0	0
Other reasons/not stated	0	0	0	25	10
Reasons for not sharing					
n injected but not shared ever	*27*	*29*	*26*	*8*	*16*
Because of AIDS	78	55	50	38	69
Because of other health risks	7	21	31	50	19
Other reasons/not stated	15	24	19	13	13

The table shows that the main reasons given for sharing needles was the absence of clean needles (25 per cent to 88 per cent of arrestees), the convenience of sharing (0 per cent to 38 per cent), or the belief that there was no health risk (0 per cent to 17 per cent). Others said that they did not think about the consequences or gave other reasons. The main reasons given for not sharing needles was the threat of AIDS (three per cent to 78 per cent of arrestees) or because of other health risks (seven per cent to 50 per cent of arrestees). The remainder gave other reasons.

Conclusion

The results of this part of the survey show that about one in five of all arrestees who have ever used heroin, methadone, cocaine, or amphetamines at some time in their lives injected the drug. The results also show that about one-third of all of those who injected the drug at some time in their lives shared needles. These findings are of some concern both in terms of the health of the arrestees who are either remanded in custody or released on bail and for the health of the police and others in the criminal justice system who regularly come into contact with what might be seen as a high health risk group.

6 Drug dependency and treatment

Introduction

The issue of drug dependency is relevant to drug testing of arrestees because the process of interviewing and specimen collection provides an opportunity to identify and possibly tackle specific problems at the point of entry into the criminal justice system. As many of these offenders are released on bail before further action is taken, there is an opportunity to provide advice or other assistance during the period between arrest and court appearance.

Drug dependency

All arrestees were asked whether they had ever been (or were currently) addicted to, or dependent on, one or more of 17 drug types. Their responses are shown in the Table 6.1 below.

The table shows that just under one-half (45%) of all arrestees said that they had been dependent upon one or more drugs (excluding alcohol) at some time in their lives. The percentage varied from one-third (33%) to two-thirds (66%) of arrestees across the five sample areas. The results also show that almost one-third (30%) of all arrestees said that they were currently dependent upon one or more drugs. This figure varied from 16 per cent (in Sunderland) to 51 per cent (in Manchester) across the five locations. Nearly one in five arrestees (18%) said that they had been dependent upon three or more drugs in their lifetime and seven per cent said that they were currently dependent upon three or more drugs. Overall, the results show that about one in three arrestees were currently dependent on one or more drug at the time of their arrest and one in 14 arrestees were currently dependent on three or more drugs.

The table also shows the prevalence of dependency among arrestees for particular drugs. Eleven per cent of arrestees said that they were dependent upon heroin at the time of arrest. This proportion varied across areas. Almost one-quarter of all arrestees in Manchester said that they were dependent on heroin at the time of arrest and over 10 per cent of arrestees in Nottingham, Cambridge, and London said that they were currently dependent upon heroin. Two per cent of all arrestees said that they were currently dependent upon cocaine and three per cent said that they currently dependent upon crack. Almost one in 10 (9%) of arrestees in Manchester said that they were dependent upon crack at the time of arrest and seven per cent were dependent upon cocaine. Just over one-fifth of detainees said that they were dependent upon cannabis a some point in their lives and 15 per cent said that they were dependent upon cannabis at the time of arrest.

Table 6.1 Percentage of arrestees dependent upon selected drugs

	Sunder-land		Notting-ham		Cam-bridge		London		Man-chester		All	
	Ever	Curr-ent	Ever	Curr-ent	Ever	Curr-ent	Ever	Curr-ent	Ever	Curr-ent	Ever	Curr-ent
	n=271		n=209		n=152		n=103		n=104		n=839	
Drug types dependent upon												
Amphetamines	14	4	16	4	28	9	3	1	30	7	18	5
Amyl nitrite	0	0	1	1	0	0	18	0	1	1	1	<1
Barbiturates	1	0	2	1	5	2	1	1	2	1	2	1
Cannabis	9	8	18	11	34	27	24	18	39	22	21	15
Cocaine	2	0	5	1	11	1	10	4	14	7	7	2
Crack	2	0	8	4	9	1	19	7	17	9	9	3
DF118s	2	0	4	1	6	1	1	1	3	2	3	1
Diazepam	8	4	8	3	7	4	7	5	14	10	4	3
Diconal	1	0	1	1	1	1	3	0	8	0	5	2
Ecstasy	4	1	4	4	11	0	1	1	8	2	6	1
Heroin	8	4	17	12	19	13	18	14	30	24	16	11
LSD	1	0	1	1	7	1	2	2	3	3	2	<1
Magic mushrooms	1	0	0	0	2	1	1	1	2	2	1	<1
Methadone	3	2	6	4	11	18	12	10	21	18	9	6
Solvents	11	0	11	1	9	0	3	3	9	2	9	1
Temazepam	9	3	9	2	11	7	5	2	9	4	9	3
Temgesic	5	2	2	1	1	1	1	1	2	2	3	1
Alcohol	27	19	27	14	30	17	24	18	20	12	26	16
Tobacco	69	66	74	69	61	59	72	69	82	81	71	68
Number of drug types dependent upon [1]												
0 drugs	67	84	59	73	43	61	52	63	34	49	55	70
1-2 drugs	25	13	23	23	30	32	33	29	34	35	28	24
3-4 drugs	4	2	11	3	15	4	10	7	20	12	10	4
5-6 drugs	2	1	4	1	6	2	5	1	7	4	4	2
7 or more drugs	3	0	3	1	6	1	1	0	6	1	4	1
1 or more drugs[2]	33	16	41	27	57	39	48	37	66	51	45	30

Notes: [1] Excluding alcohol and tobacco;

[2] The percentages do not always add to 100% due to rounding.

The results of the research suggest that drug dependency is fairly common among arrestees and just under one in three respondents said that they were dependent on at least one drug at the time of interview. These results have obvious implications for methods of dealing with arrestees. One possible implication is that some kind of treatment for drug dependency is recommended or made available for arrestees. One way of doing this is to refer arrestees (who are released) to existing treatment sources. However, it is not clear what kinds of treatment would be most appropriate and what kinds of treatment would be most acceptable to drug-dependent arrestees. During the interviews, arrestees were asked about what kinds of treatment for drug abuse they had received in the past and what kinds of treatment they would like to receive in the future.

Treatment

The following table shows the proportion of arrestees who had received treatment for drug dependency in the past and the proportion who thought that they needed treatment. One in five arrestees said that they had received some kind of treatment for drug dependence in the past and about the same proportion said that they would like to receive treatment at the current time. Those who said that they would like treatment were fairly evenly divided among those who had received treatment in the past and those who had not received treatment in the past.

Table 6.2 Percentage of arrestees who had received treatment for drug dependence in the past and who would currently like treatment for drug dependence

	Sunder-land n=271	Notting-ham n=209	Cam-bridge n=152	London n=103	Man-chester n=104	All n=839
Treatment for drug dependence received in the past	13	21	24	21	31	20
Treatment received in the past Treatment for drug dependence currently wanted	8	13	15	16	24	13
Treatment not received in the past Treatment for drug dependence currently wanted	7	5	13	14	11	9
All Treatment for drug dependence currently wanted	15	18	28	30	35	22

Table 6.3 shows the kinds of treatment received in the past and wanted in the future. About one-fifth of arrestees in Manchester had received treatment from a drug clinic at some time in the past and about one in 10 arrestees in Nottingham, Cambridge, and London had attended drug clinics in their lifetime. About one-fifth of arrestees in London and Manchester said that they would like to attend a drug clinic for treatment relating to their dependency. Arrestees in Sunderland and Nottingham were asked about the kinds of treatment that they would like to receive (this question was not included in earlier versions of the questionnaire). A small proportion of arrestees said that they preferred some form of maintenance or stabilisation prescribing of the drugs of their addiction. However, a larger proportion of arrestees said that they wanted help in coming off drugs (seven per cent in Sunderland and nine per cent in Nottingham). The remainder wanted other kinds of help including counselling and individual and group therapy.

Table 6.3 Source of treatment and kinds of treatment for drug dependence received in the past and currently wanted
Percentages

	Sunder-land n=271	Notting-ham n=209	Cam-bridge n=152	London n=103	Man-chester n=104
Source of treatment for drug dependence					
Received in the past					
Drug clinic	3	12	13	9	20
General practitioner	1	4	8	5	12
Private practitioner	0	1	2	3	0
Hospital in-patient	4	2	1	0	3
Other	3	6	5	4	1
Currently wanted					
Drug clinic	6	9	12,	17	20
General practitioner	4	3	8	6	11
Private practitioner	1	1	3	0	1
Hospital in-patient	3	1	4	2	7
Other	3	3	9	7	11
Type of treatment for drug dependence					
Received in the past					
Withdrawal	5	10	*	*	*
Maintenance	<1	5	*	*	*
Counselling	5	10	*	*	*
Therapy (group)	1	2	*	*	*
Therapy (individual)	1	4	*	*	*
Other	4	1	*	*	*
Currently wanted					
Withdrawal	7	9	*	*	*
Maintenance	2	3	*	*	*
Counselling	6	8	*	*	*
Therapy (group)	3	3	*	*	*
Therapy (individual)	3	2	*	*	*
Other	2	3	*	*	*

Notes: Includes multiple responses. An '*' represents a non-response and is a result of the related questions not being
        included in the first three surveys.

Conclusion

Overall, the impression given by these results is that a large proportion of arrestees are currently dependent upon one or more illegal drugs and that many of these would like help in dealing with the problems of drug abuse. The findings do not support the contention that arrestees merely wanted treatment as a means of obtaining drugs. Arrestees were given various options for type of treatment currently wanted, including maintenance prescribing (being prescribed drugs on prescription) and withdrawal (not being prescribed drugs on prescription). Three times as many arrestees chose the withdrawal option as the maintenance options.

These findings suggest that there might be an opportunity to provide treatment advice or to make available some kind of treatment programme to arrestees at the point of contact with the criminal justice system. Many arrestees are charged and bailed and returned to the community without finding an opportunity to discuss their drug dependency or treatment needs. The point of arrest and the subsequent period of official processing taps into this high-risk group of people for a short period of time (see Edmunds et al., 1998, for a discussion of recent arrest-referral schemes).

7. Lifestyle addendum

Introduction

During the last two years the DUF Program in the United States has begun using a number 'addendum' questionnaires which ask a broader range of questions. These new questions aim to extend the use of arrestee sampling by dealing with additional issues that may be of particular relevance when monitored over time. New questions that have been shown to have been particularly useful concern questions on place and method of purchasing drugs. Information from these surveys has been used to help explain the reduction in crime rate in New York City over the last few years. The surveys have shown not only a reduction in cocaine use (in relation to drug testing of arrestees), but also a reduction of street (outdoors) drug dealing and an increase in indoors drug dealing. Other new questions have been added to monitor changes in gun ownership among different kinds of arrestees over time and to collect information on offender lifestyles, including medical and housing problems.

As part of the last two surveys in Nottingham and Sunderland, new 'addendum-styled' questions were added to the questionnaire. These included questions on: sources of drugs, gun ownership, health, living conditions, and recent involvement with the criminal justice system.

Sources of illegal drugs

It is possible that prevention methods that aim to disrupt open street dealing should (if successful) inhibit the ability of users to buy locally, to buy outdoors, and to contact a choice of dealers. Table 7.1 provides some information on the method and ease of drug purchase among arrestees in Nottingham and Sunderland.

Over half of crack/cocaine users in Nottingham and Sunderland (50% and 58% respectively) and over half of heroin users (60% and 77% respectively) said that they were able to buy their drugs locally (i.e. in the neighbourhood in which they lived). Hence, drugs were fairly easy to obtain locally in these locations and did not require users to travel out of their area to obtain them. About half of crack/cocaine users in Nottingham (45%) were able to buy their drugs outdoors compared with 19 per cent of crack/cocaine users in Sunderland. A similar proportion of heroin users in Nottingham (44%) were able to buy their drugs outdoors compared with 31 per cent of heroin users in Sunderland. The table also shows that crack/cocaine users in Nottingham had contact with a higher mean number of dealers (10.3) than in Sunderland (7.5). However, heroin users in Nottingham had a smaller mean number of dealers (13.8) than heroin users in Sunderland (18.4).

Table 7.1 Source of drug purchases among cocaine/crack and heroin users in the last 12 months
Percentages

	Sunderland		Nottingham	
	Crack/ cocaine users n=44	Heroin users n=28	Crack/ cocaine users n=58	Heroin users n=50
Buy in own neighbourhood				
Yes	58	77	50	60
No	42	23	50	40
Total	100	100	100	100
Buy indoors or outdoors				
Indoors	81	69	55	56
Outdoors	19	31	45	44
Total	100	100	100	100
Mean number of dealers available	7.5	18.4	10.3	13.8

Notes: Percentages have been calculated on the total number of respondents stating that they had used the respective drugs within the last 12 months.

The results suggest that the market for heroin is somewhat more active (in terms of ability to buy locally, to buy outdoors, and to buy from a large number of dealers) in both areas than the market for cocaine. This may be a result of difference in police operations or other factors which constrain the cocaine markets in comparison with the heroin markets.

The results of this part of the research provide useful baseline measures relating to drug dealing. However, the data would be even more useful (and are primarily designed to be used) as a measure of changes in drug dealing characteristics of the area when compared over time. It is hoped that future research can address these issues.

Gun ownership

Information on ownership and access to guns among arrestees could be used to identify changes in the seriousness of offending and the way in which this might vary in relation to different types of crime or to different types of offenders. In common with all the 'addendum' questions, the data collected are most useful when compared over time. Information on gun ownership would be useful in monitoring the effect of recent changes in the law relating to legal gun ownership and the extent that these changes impacted on illegal gun ownership. An early warning of an increase in gun ownership and access among arrestees would be important information which could be used to alert the police of potential changes in the nature of criminal behaviour in an area and to assist them in devising preventative strategies.

In the surveys in Nottingham and Sunderland, all arrestees were asked whether they had ever owned or had access to a gun and (if so) whether they had owned or had access to a gun in the last 12 months. The responses relating to 'owning' a gun and 'having access to - but not owning' a gun were recorded separately. The following table provides baseline data on gun ownership and access in these two survey areas. Table 7.2 shows that over one-quarter of arrestees in Nottingham (28%) and over one-third of arrestees in Sunderland (37%) said that they had owned or had access to a gun at some time in their lives. Just under one-fifth of arrestees in Nottingham (17%) and just under one-quarter of arrestees in Sunderland (23%) said that they currently owned or had access to a gun. One in 12 arrestees (8%) in Nottingham and one in 33 arrestees in Sunderland (3%) said that they currently owned a gun. In both areas, males were more likely than females to say that they currently or had ever owned or had access to a gun. In neither area was there a clear association between age and access to a gun or ownership of a gun.

It is difficult to know how to evaluate this information as there are no baseline measures on which to draw and no other surveys of this kind with which to make a comparison. It was not possible within the time constraints of the interviews to probe further into issues relating to gun ownership. It would have been useful to know something about the type of gun involved and whether it was a hand gun or shot gun, or automatic or semi-automatic. It is possible that some guns may have been owned legally for sports purposes and it is also possible that some arrestees had served time in the armed forces and had legal access to weapons. Nevertheless, the results of the current research suggest that there is at least a potential problem in relation to gun ownership and access and future research on arrestees might investigate this issue further.

Table 7.2 Percentage of arrestees owning or having access to a gun

	Sunderland Ever n=271	Recently	Nottingham Ever n=209	Recently
Owned a gun	9	3	13	8
Had access to a gun	16	14	15	9
Both owned and had access to a gun	12	6	0	0
Neither owned nor had access to a gun	63	77	72	83
Total	100	100	100	100

Health

The third table concerns the state of health and other health issues relating to the sample of arrestees. Information about health and disease is important in identifying the health problems and needs of individual detainees and it is also important in identifying potential health risks to people (such as the police) who come into contact with them. It would also be valuable to monitor this information across areas and over time to observe the way in which the situation varies.

The table shows that five of the 209 arrestees in Nottingham (2%) and two of the 271 arrestees in Sunderland (1%) knew or believed that they had AIDS or were HIV positive. Seventeen per cent of arrestees in Nottingham and seven per cent of arrestees in Sunderland said that people they mixed with had AIDS or were HIV positive. Four per cent of arrestees in Nottingham (but no arrestees in Sunderland) said that they had had hepatitis either currently or at some point in their lives. Fourteen per cent of the sample in Nottingham and four per cent of the sample in Sunderland said that they mixed with people who had hepatitis currently or at some time in the past.

Table 7.3 Percentage of arrestees with AIDS or Hepatitis

	Sunderland n=271	Nottingham n=209
Knows or believes he or she has AIDS	1	2
Knows or believes at least one friend has AIDS	7	17
Knows or believes he or she has Hepatitis	0	4
Knows or believes at least one friend has Hepatitis	4	14

These results show that about two per cent of arrestees in Nottingham and one per cent of arrestees in Sunderland passing through the custody block had AIDS or were HIV positive (on average, about one arrestee every second or third day in the case of Nottingham). They also represent a health risk to the police and other employees of the criminal justice system who handle arrestees (especially when their illness is connected with intravenous drug use and when there is a risk of needles being held in the possession of the arrestee at the time of search).

Living conditions

The next two tables in this section concern accommodation and living problems faced by arrestees. While there is little research evidence on the effect of homelessness on desistance from criminal behaviour or drug use, it is possible that offenders who have temporary or unsatisfactory accommodation (especially those living rough) will find it harder to terminate offending and drug use than others who have more permanent and more satisfactory accommodation.

Table 7.4 Place of residence and number of places lived in the last 12 months
Percentage

	Sunderland n=271	Nottingham n=209
Lived in more than one place in the last 12 months	46	63
Mean number of places lived in the last 12 months		
All	2.3	3.6
Those who lived in more than one place	3.7	5.2
	n= 126	n= 131
Mean number of places lived in the last 30 days		
All	1.4	1.4
Those who lived in more than one place	2.6	3.2
	n= 28	n= 40

The first table shows that almost two-thirds of arrestees in Nottingham (63%) and almost half of arrestees in Sunderland (46%) lived in more than one place in the 12-month period prior to the current arrest. On average, the sample of arrestees as a whole lived in 3.6 places in the Nottingham sample and 2.3 places in the Sunderland sample. In the last 30 days, the sample as a whole in both survey areas lived in 1.4 places and those who lived in more than one place lived, on average, in 3.2 places (Nottingham) and 2.6 places (Sunderland).

Table 7.5 Number of nights spent on the street in the last 12 months
Percentage

	Sunderland n=271	Nottingham n=209
Lived on the streets in the last 12 months	10	15
Mean number of nights spent on the streets in the last 12 months		
All	2	13
Those who lived on the street	18	89
	n= 27	n= 31

The second table shows that 13 per cent of all arrestees in Nottingham and two per cent of all arrestees in Sunderland lived on the streets for some of the time in the last 12 months. Those who lived on the streets for at least some of the time in the last 12 months, lived rough for an average of 89 nights (among the Nottingham sample) and 18 nights (among the Sunderland sample).

Involvement with the criminal justice system

The final table concerns involvement with the criminal justice system. The table shows that over half of arrestees in Sunderland and Nottingham reported that they had been arrested at least once before in the last 12 months. About one-fifth of arrestees in Sunderland and one-quarter of arrestees in Nottingham had served some time in prison in the last 12 months.

Table 7.6 Percentage of arrestees with involvement with the criminal justice system in the last 12 months

	Sunderland n=271	Nottingham n=209
Arrested at least once before in the last 12 months	52	58
Served time in prison in the last 12 months	22	25

Conclusion

One of the aims of the lifestyle and other addendum questionnaires used in the DUF Program in the United States is to extend the value of monitoring of arrestees beyond determining immediate prevalence figures for drug use.

The point of contact with a representative sample of arrestees provides an opportunity to monitor a large number of factors relating to this sample for comparisons across areas and across time. The current survey has used only some of the questions used in the DUF Program. However, it has shown that useful monitoring information can be collected about arrestee populations.

The survey results obtained in the first two surveys in which these 'addendum' questions were included have shown that arrestees find it fairly easy to obtain their sources of drugs. They also report making purchases both indoors and outdoors and having access to a good supply of dealers. There is an alarmingly high proportion of arrestees who have access to, or own, guns which would be particularly important to monitor over time and to compare across areas. Arrestees are more likely than the general population to have AIDS or to have contracted hepatitis. Arrestees tend to move their place of residence often and 10 per cent or more of them occasionally or permanently live rough on the streets. The majority of arrestees have experienced recent contact with the criminal justice system (in addition to the current contact) either in terms of recent arrest or recent imprisonment.

8 Discussion

Emerging issues

The study is the first attempt in this country to use drug testing to monitor drug use among arrestees. The results of the urinalysis and of the interviews with arrestees have shown high levels of drug use. With the exception of cocaine use, drug use prevalence figures in the five survey sites in England are as high, or higher, than those shown in the 23 survey sites of the DUF Program in the United States. The results suggest that drug use in this country is an integral part of the lifestyle of the most common types of offender.

The study has identified a number of key findings which might need to be addressed in the future. The main finding is the high prevalence rate of drug use among arrestees. Two out of three of all arrestees across quite different research sites tested positive for at least one drug (excluding alcohol). One in five arrestees tested positive for opiates and one in 10 tested positive for cocaine (including 'crack'). These high drug-use prevalence rates among arrestees are also reflected in the estimates of the prevalence rate of drug use in relation to particular offence types. The research has shown that almost half of arrestees suspected of shoplifting across the five survey areas tested positive for opiates and about one-third tested positive for cocaine. About 10 per cent of all suspected burglars and one-quarter of all suspected car thieves tested positive for opiates.

A second key finding which has broader implications and significance is the strong observed correlation between drug use and criminal behaviour. Drug use appears to be part of the lifestyle of a large proportion of arrestees. It cannot be determined conclusively from the current research design whether crime would reduce if drug use were reduced. However, if it were assumed that the two were causally connected, then the evidence suggests that a reduction in the use of the most addictive and expensive forms of drug use would lead to significant reductions in income-generating crime.

Another important issue which emerged from the research, and which might be monitored across areas and over time, concerns drug use and health. The results showed that one in five arrestees had injected drugs at some time in their lives and one in seven had done so in the last 12 months. The study also showed that about one-third of all arrestees who had injected drugs had shared needles. Intravenous injection of illegal drugs is a problem both for the arrestee whose health is at risk and for those who regularly come into contact with arrestees and who may handle their drug-use paraphernalia.

Another finding which might have broader implications is the high level of dependency on drugs reported by arrestees. As a result, about one-fifth of all arrestees reported that they would like help in dealing with their dependency.

Other issues concern the general lifestyles of arrestees. A high proportion of arrestees said that they had access to guns. A small proportion of arrestees reported serious health problems in relation to AIDS and hepatitis and many arrestees did not have stable living accommodation. At least 10 per cent of arrestees had spent some time living rough on the streets in the 12-month period before interview. The majority of arrestees had recent contact with the criminal justice system and about one-quarter had served recent prison sentences.

Overall, these findings suggest that arrestees experience a wide range of social and individual problems which are of concern, not just to them, but also to society as a whole. At the moment, with some notable exceptions, arrestees come into contact with the criminal justice system and are released again (either immediately or eventually) without any of these problems being addressed.

Arrestee monitoring as an alternative measure of drug use

Systematic monitoring of arrestees for recent drug misuse has been a regular feature of research on drug use in the United States since the inception of the DUF Program in the late 1980s. However, there has been no comparable research on arrestees in England and Wales and little has been known about the drug-using profiles (and many other characteristics) of arrestees in this country.

There are a number of indicators of drug use which are currently being used to monitor trends in drug use. These include: (1) large-scale surveys of the general population at a national or regional level; (2) official data on selected sub-groups of the general population at a national or regional level; and (3) small-scale research studies on either the general population of specific drug-using or criminal sub-groups. The most important indicators of drug use within these categories until recently have been: (1) prevalence rates within the general population measured by the British Crime Surveys; (2) official statistics on (a) convictions for drug offences and (b) drug seizures; (3) official statistics on notification by general practitioners and other medical practitioners of addicts and suspected addicts (although the Addicts' Index has recently been disbanded); and (4) data on treatment for drug problems held on Drug Misuse Databases.

There are a number of problems with the main national-level indicators of drug use. Surveys of the general population do not tap sufficiently well the small proportion of high-rate users in the country who determine national trends and local problems. Surveys of criminal populations through enforcement data deal only with drug offences, either in terms of convictions for drug offences or in terms of seizures of drugs. This means that there are no national-level and regularly-collected indicators of drug use relating to the criminal population as a whole. Surveys of arrestees (particularly national surveys) have the advantage that they tap a potential criminal population at the point of entry into the criminal justice system and at a point typically soon after the commission of an offence. Arrestee monitoring has the potential to provide useful information about trends in drug use among this criminal population over time and across different geographic areas.

Arrestee monitoring and targeted intervention

The original aim of the DUF Program in the United States was to identify trends in drug use and trends in drug-related crime which could be detected early enough to devise effective intervention strategies.

Drug testing and interviewing representative samples of arrestees can help generate local-level profiles of drug use which might inform intervention strategies, both at a point in time and in preparation for any emerging trends. The current research in five survey areas has shown that particular areas have particular drug-use profiles. For example, the areas covered by the surveys in London and Manchester generated a profile which showed a high prevalence of cocaine and crack use and low levels of amphetamine and alcohol use. The areas covered by the surveys in Sunderland showed almost the opposite picture with low levels of cocaine and crack use and high levels of alcohol use. The survey in Cambridge showed high levels of opiate and amphetamine use. Clearly, the kinds of intervention strategies devised in these areas might be most effective if they reflected the nature of drug use within them.

The above argument is based on an assumption, which as yet has not been tested, that there is a correlation between the drug-use profiles of arrestees in a particular area and the drug-using profile more generally of the area. There are a number of reasons to expect that this is true. The DUF Program literature argues that arrestees comprise the most active end of the drug use and criminal behaviour spectrum and may be responsible for a high proportion of both drug use and crime. It also argues that arrestees will be the first groups to try new drugs and to exploit new drug markets. While these arguments are all very plausible, it has to be acknowledged that there has been no research done in this country which can prove this. If research shows these assumptions to be correct, then drug use among arrestees would be an extremely useful and efficient means of measuring drug use locally among the populations as a whole (including arrestees and non-arrestees). This information could then be used to devise appropriate intervention strategies.

Arrestee monitoring as an alternative measure of crime

The argument that arrestee monitoring can be used as an alternative measure of crime follows the previous argument very closely. The current research has shown that the crime profiles of arrestees (the crimes that they are suspected of committing) also varies across areas. For example, the proportion of alcohol-related offences (drunk-driving, disorder, criminal damage) was much higher in some areas (e.g. Nottingham and Sunderland) than in others (e.g. Cambridge).

These differences would already be known to the local police and can be determined from crime analysis of reported crimes. However, arrestee monitoring can supplement information derived from reported crime in various ways. Arrestee monitoring can be used to measure changing characteristics of the criminal population including analysing the criminal histories of arrestees and their individual characteristics such as age and drug involvement. It might also be possible to assess changes in the seriousness of offending by, for example, changes in reported ownership of guns (which could be extended to include knives and other weapons).

However, the main reason for including a section on the relationship between arrestee monitoring and crime is that one of the original aims of the DUF Program was to predict crime trends and changes in crime. It was believed that drug testing and interviewing arrestees could be used to identify early changes in drug use and (once the connection between drugs and crime was understood more fully) it could be used to predict the effects of these changes on drug-related crime. If it were the case that changes in drug use preceded changes in crime, then it would be possible to take actions to deal with the change in crime before it happened (and perhaps prevent it from happening). There is some evidence from research that increases in cocaine use across various states in North America preceded increases in robbery in those states (Baumer, 1994; NIJ, 1997[b]).

Arrestee monitoring as a method of programme evaluation

The establishment of Drug Action Teams has resulted in an expansion of local programmes which have attempted to prevent or modify in some way local drug use. It might also be possible to use the results of arrestee monitoring to measure the effectiveness of some of these programmes. However, it would first have to be established that drug-use profiles among arrestees mirror (or correlate in some known way) to drug-use profiles of the wider community from which they are drawn. For example, it would have to be established that prevalence of drug use among arrestees was correlated with prevalence of drug use at the community level (and when drug use at the community level reduced, drug use at the arrestee level reduced). Unfortunately, there is no research in this country which can be brought to bear on this issue.

Some drug-prevention programmes could also be evaluated using other information collected during the arrestee interviews. It was argued in the previous chapter that changes in the ability of arrestees to buy drugs locally, to buy outdoors, and to use a number of dealers might by used as evidence for the effectiveness of policing strategies which aimed to disrupt local drug markets.

Arrestee monitoring might also be used to evaluate programmes relating directly to the treatment of arrestees. Some police forces have developed referral schemes whereby arrestees who are thought to have drug use problems are encouraged to contact local agencies. It is possible that the effectiveness of these programmes could be evaluated by regular monitoring of arrestees.

Arrestee drug abuse monitoring in Britain

The results of the current research suggest that there might be much to be gained from developing a national system of arrestee drug abuse monitoring in Britain. It could provide an important additional indicator of drug use nationally among a sub-section of the population who are possibly the most likely to be involved in drug use and who might be particularly active in determining the character and direction of the most damaging kinds of drug use in the country as a whole. It could also provide some of the means discussed above for generating other important mechanisms for monitoring drug use, such as: an early indication of incipient changes in drug use and in drug-related crime; a means of profiling areas and targeting interventions; and a possible way of evaluating the effectiveness of drug-use reduction strategies.

In one sense the time is right to do this because of the expansion of the DUF Program in the United States. In 1997, the DUF Program changed its name to ADAM (Arrestee Drug Abuse Monitoring) in line with other changes in its method of operation and its procedures. One of the main philosophical changes has been to broaden the programme from its early focus on drug use prevalence among arrestees to a broader range of aspects of the characteristics and behaviour of arrestees and assessing the likely impact of these changes on crime (e.g. monitoring gun use). As part of this change, the National Institute of Justice has set up a structure to enable international collaboration in relation to monitoring of arrestees called I-ADAM (International Arrestee Drug Abuse Monitoring Program). The aim of I-ADAM is to monitor arrestees internationally in order to share knowledge and to identify larger-scale international trends which might provide knowledge and aid prevention. Britain could play a part in this international development by generating its own national programme of arrestee drug abuse monitoring .

Arrestee drug abuse monitoring has, to date, been implemented within a research context and it would be expected that future developments in Britain and elsewhere would also be based on this context. Drug testing of arrestees within the DUF Program and within the current research has been voluntary and based on confidentiality and a separation of interests of the researcher and the criminal justice process. Research of this kind has to be bound by research ethics and the accepted routines of research procedures. It requires the co-operation of a number of agencies, including the police and the Crown Prosecution Service, and care must be taken to observe the letter and the spirit of the Police and Criminal Evidence Act (1984). It would be unwise to implement similar procedures outside of a research context and without careful consideration of these issues. However, within such a context, the current research has shown that arrestee drug abuse monitoring can provide an effective and informative indicator of a range of aspects of drug misuse and criminal behaviour.

References

Baumer, E. (1994) 'Poverty, crack, and crime: a cross-city analysis', *Journal of Research in Crime and Delinquency*, 31, pp.311-327.

Bennett, T.H. (1991) 'Drug Use and Criminal Behaviour'. In: I.B. Glass (ed.) *The International Handbook of Addiction Behaviour*. London: Routledge.

Bennett, T.H. (1995) *A Feasibility Study of Drug Testing of Arrestees in England and Wales*. Cambridge: Institute of Criminology.

Bennett, T.H. (1997a) *Drug Testing of Arrestees in England and Wales: The Effect of Convenience Sampling on the Representativeness of the Results obtained in Cambridge*. Cambridge: Institute of Criminology.

Bennett, T.H. (1997b) *Drug Testing of Arrestees in England and Wales: The Effect of Convenience Sampling on the Representativeness of the Results obtained in Hammersmith*. Cambridge: Institute of Criminology.

Chatterton, M., Gibson, G., Gilman, M., Godfrey, D., Sutton, M. and Wright, A. (1995) *Performance Indicators for Local Anti-Drugs Strategies: A Preliminary Analysis*. Police Research Group Crime Detection and Prevention Series: Paper No.62. London: Home Office.

Decker, S.H. (1992) *Drug Use Forecasting in St. Louis: A Three Year Report*. St Louis, Missouri: Department of Criminology and Criminal Justice, University of Missouri-St. Louis.

Edmunds, M., May, T., Hearnden, I., and Hough, M. (1998) *Arrest Referral: Emerging Lessons from Research*, Drugs Prevention Paper 23. London. Home Office.

Frischer, M. (1992) 'Estimating prevalence of injecting drug use in Glasgow', *British Journal of Addiction*, 87, pp.235-243.

Leitner, M., Shapland, J. and Wiles, P. (1993) *Drug Usage and Drugs Prevention: The Views and Habits of the General Public*. London: HMSO.

Maden, A., Swinton, M. and Gunn, J. (1992) 'A survey of pre-arrest drug use in sentenced prisoners', *British Journal of Addiction*, 87, pp.27-33.

NIJ (1991) *Edward Byrne Memorial State and Local Law Enforcement Assistance Program: Discretionary Program Application Kit*. Washington D.C. U.S. Department of Justice.

NIJ (1996) *Drug Use Forecasting: 1995: Annual Report on Adult and Juvenile Arrestees*. Washington D.C.: U.S. Department of Justice.

NIJ (1997[a]) *Drug Use Forecasting: 1996 Annual Report on Adult and Juvenile Arrestees*. Washington D.C.: U.S. Department of Justice.

NIJ (1997[b]) *A Study of Homicide in Eight U.S. Cities: An NIJ Intramural Research Project*. Research in Brief (November). Washington D.C.: U.S. Department of Justice.

Power, K.G., Markova, A., Rowlands, K., McKee, K.J., Anslow, P.J., and Kilfedder, D. (1992) 'Intravenous drug use and HIV transmission amongst inmates in Scottish prisons', *British Journal of Addiction*, 87, pp.35-45.

Ramsay, M. and Spiller, J. (1997) *Drug Misuse Declared in 1996: Latest Results from the British Crime Survey*. Home Office Research Study 172. London: Home Office.

Riley, J. (1996) Personal communication.

Riley, J. (Undated) *International Arrestee Drug Abuse Monitoring Program*. Washington. D.C.: NIJ.

Robertson, G., Gibb, R. And Pearson, R. (1995) 'Drunkenness among police detainees', *Addiction*, 90, pp.793-803.

Wish, E.D. and Gropper, B.A. (1990) 'Drug testing by the criminal justice system: methods, research, and applications'. In: M. Tonry and J.Q. Wilson, *Drugs and Crime*. London: The University of Chicago Press.

Appendix A: Sample and population characteristics

The following tables summarise information relating to the sampling and the sample characteristics. Table A.1 provides a breakdown of the sex, age, and race characteristics of the interview sample and the specimen sample in relation to the population of all arrestees processed through the custody blocks of the five survey areas during the period of the survey (ranging from one month in Nottingham and Sunderland to four months in Cambridge).

Table A.1 Sample and arrestee population by sex, age, and race by location
Percentages [1]

	Sex Males	Females	Age 16-20	21-30	31 or more	Race White	Non-white
Sunderland							
Interview sample n=271	87	13	36	43	21	98	2
Specimen sample n=209	88	12	35	42	23	99	1
Population n=635 [2]	86	14	36	38	26	98	2
Nottingham							
Interview sample n=209	79	21	23	50	27	90	10 ** [4]
Specimen sample n=132	83	17	26	48	26	94	6 ***
Population n=781	74	26	25	45	30	81	19
Cambridge							
Interview sample n=152	89	11	35	43	22	84	16
Specimen sample n=124	94	7	34	43	23	87	13
Population n=2,156	88	12	31	39	29	-	-
London							
Interview sample n=103	88	12	30	34	35	47	53 ***
Specimen sample n=79	92	8	31	27	42	47	53 ***
Population n=1,023	90	10	26	34	40	66	34
Manchester							
Interview sample n=104	90	10	29	47	24	91	9
Specimen sample n=77	90	10	28	50	22	92	9
Population n=313 [3]	88	12	28	38	34	92	8
Total							
Interview sample n=839	86	14	31	44	25	87	13
Specimen sample n=621	88	12	31	43	26	88	12

Notes: [1] The percentages are valid percentages and exclude missing values;
[2] The percentage distribution of the population in relation to age for all survey areas was based on arrestees aged 16 and over;
[3] Data on the population of arrestees was not obtained in the one of the two sites surveyed in Manchester. The percentages shown refer to the single site for which data were obtained;
[4] ***=Significant at p<.001, **=Signficant at p<.01.

The table shows that, with just two exceptions in Nottingham and two exceptions in London, there were no significant differences between the interview and specimen samples and the population from which they were drawn in terms of sex, age or race of the arrestee. The four significant differences shown in the table all relate to the race of the respondent. In London, non-white arrestees were over-represented in both the interview and the specimen samples in comparison with the population. In Nottingham, non-white arrestees were under-represented in both the interview and the specimen sample in comparison with the population.

The former significant difference is hard to explain as the survey was done in the earlier stage of the research before systematic data on eligibility and reasons for non-response were collected on all arrestees (which was introduced with the change to probability sampling half-way through the study). The early stage of the research was modelled on the DUF Program in the United States which operated a system of convenience sampling and which did not require collecting information on the population of arrestees (although some recent analyses have been done by independent researchers). It is known from analyses conducted for earlier interim reports relating to the project that before the change to probability sampling most arrestees were selected and interviewed during the day. This means that detainees arrested in the evening or overnight were under-represented in the samples. It is possible that white detainees were more likely than non-white detainees to be arrested in the evening or overnight which would serve to under-represent this group in the final samples. There is some circumstantial evidence to support this. Detainees arrested during the evening and over-night were more likely to be involved in alcohol-related offences such as drunkenness offences, drink-driving offences, criminal damage, and disorderly behaviour. Detainees arrested during the evening were significantly more likely to test positive for alcohol. White arrestees in London were more likely than non-white arrestees to test positive for alcohol (see Appendix D., Table D.3). However, in the absence of the kind of data collected as part of the change to probability sampling which identified that nature of losses at each stage in the sampling process, it is not possible to identify conclusively the cause for the sample and population differences.

The latter significant difference is easier to explain as the survey was done during the latter stage of the research using probability sampling and systematic data collection on reasons for non-response. Details relating to the various sampling stages and the reasons for non-responses at each stage in relation to Nottingham are shown in Table A.2 in relation to sex, age, and race. The table shows that there was no difference in the proportion of white and non-white arrestees who were initially approached for interview (52 per cent of eligible white arrestees and 49 per cent of eligible non-white arrestees). There was also no difference in the distribution of reasons for approaching one group compared with another. However, there was a significant difference in the proportion of white and non-white arrestees approached who were eventually interviewed. Eighty-seven per cent of white detainees who were approached were eventually interviewed compared with 64 per cent of non-white arrestees. The main reasons for the difference in response was the higher proportion of non-white arrestees who refused to be interviewed. There was also a significant difference in the proportion of white and non-white arrestees who were willing to provide a urine specimen at the end of the interview. Sixty-eight per cent of white detainees compared with 44 per cent of non-white arrestees agreed to give a urine specimen. The main reason for the difference was again the higher refusal rate among non-white arrestees.

Table A.2 Sample and arrestee population by sex, age, and race: Nottingham Percentages

	Sex		Age			Race	
	Males	Females	16-20	21-30	31 or more	White	Non-white
% of those eligible who were approached	54	44	54	54	47	52	49
Reasons for not approaching							
No custody staff available	4	1	0	6	1	4	0
Researcher with another detainee	9	13	7	12	9	9	15
No researcher on duty at the time	1	0	0	0	1	0	0
Researcher unavailable at the time	1	0	2	0	1	0	0
Detainee in custody for a short time	65	67	66	65	68	66	59
Custody staff thought it inappropriate	1	3	0	1	4	2	2
Other reasons/missing	20	16	25	17	16	19	24
Total	101	100	100	101	100	100	100
% of those approached who were interviewed	85	78	88	83	82	87	64 ***
Reasons for not interviewing							
Detainee refused	83	73	67	91	58	70	93
Other/missing	17	27	33	9	42	30	7
Total	100	100	100	100	100	100	100
% of those interviewed who provided a specimen	67	55	74	60	66	68	44 *
Reasons for not obtaining specimen							
Detainee refused	86	69	70	83	84	79	92
Detainee unsuccessful	14	31	30	17	16	21	8
Total	100	100	100	100	100	100	100

Notes: *=p<.05; **=p<.01; ***=p<.001.

The following four tables provide summary information on the various sampling stages in relation to Nottingham and Sunderland (the two survey areas based on probability sampling). The first table (Table A.3) shows the reasons why detainees processed by the police were not deemed to be eligible to be approached for interview. In the case of Nottingham, additional eligibility criteria were included to deal with the problem that the bridewell serviced the magistrate's court next door, which resulted in a higher than usual number of detainees held in custody for very short periods of time while awaiting court appearance. Hence, four categories of reasons for custody (unrelated to suspicion of commission of an offence) were excluded from the outset. In Sunderland, a relatively small number of arrestees were held for these four reasons and they were not excluded from the outset (although few were approached and interviewed because of the short time that they were held in custody). Table A.3 shows that most of the detainees deemed to be ineligible due to reasons relating to custody were 'answering bail'. Most of the detainees who were ineligible due to conditions relating to the arrestee were children or juveniles. The second highest category of exclusion in Nottingham (but not in Sunderland) was that the detainee was unfit to be interviewed. It is possible that the rejection of detainees for reasons relating to being unfit due to alcohol or drugs serves to underestimate the level of alcohol and drug involvement among the sample selected. The relatively higher rates of rejection of arrestees in Nottingham compared with Sunderland as a result of being unfit is perhaps a result of the location of the Nottingham custody suite which was inside the town centre.

The second table (Table A.4) gives the breakdown of reasons relating to the initial approach for interview. The table shows that a proportion of all detainees eligible to be approached for interview were not approached by a researcher. The main reasons for not approaching an eligible arrestee were that the detainee was in custody for a short time only or that the researcher was with another detainees at the time. The third table (Table A.5) concerns the proportion of detainees who were approached for interview who were not interviewed. The table shows that the main reason given for not interviewing a detainee who had been approached was that the detainee refused. The fourth table (Table A.6) concerns the proportion of arrestees who were interviewed who did not provide a specimen. The table shows that the main reason for not providing a specimen was refusal. The remaining reason for not collecting a specimen was that the arrestee agreed to provide one, but was unable to do so at the time.

Table A.3 Reasons why detainees were ineligible

	Nottingham	Sunderland
	n	n
Total detainees processed	781	635
Total Ineligible		
(A) Concerning reasons for custody		
Answering bail	108	
Warrant- FTA	91	
Warrant-Other	9	
Breach-Various	4	
Sub-Total	212	
(B) Concerning condition of arrestee		
Unfit-alcohol/ drugs	65	13
Mentally disordered	6	18
Children/juveniles	80	144
Required interpreter	1	3
Potentially violent	6	8
At staff discretion	2	7
Other	3	34
Missing	*	11
Sub-Total	163	238
Total	375	238

Table A.4 Reasons for not requesting an interview from eligible detainees

	Nottingham		Sunderland	
Total eligible to be approached for interview	406		397	
Total detainees approached by interviewer	246		311	
Total not approached by interviewer	160		86	
Reasons for not requesting an interview	n	Valid % (exc. missing)	n	Valid % (exc. missing)
No custody staff available	6	4	0	0
Researcher with another detainee at the time	19	13	36	42
No researcher on duty at the time	1	1	1	1
Researcher unavailable at the time	1	1	5	6
Detainee in custody for a short time only	92	63	34	40
Custody staff thought it inappropriate	5	3	1	1
Detainee asleep at the time	4	3	0	0
Interviewed by police/solicitor at the time	3	2	0	0
Interviewed by researchers previously	7	5	0	0
Baby or child present	2	1	0	0
Interviewer felt uncomfortable with detainee	2	1	0	0
Other reasons	3	2	9	10
Missing	15	-	0	-
Total	160	99	86	100

Table A.5 Reasons for not interviewing detainees approached

	Nottingham		Sunderland	
Total approached by interviewer	246		311	
Total interviewed	209		271	
Total not interviewed	37		40	
Reasons for not interviewing	n	Valid % (exc. missing)	n	Valid % (exc. missing)
Detainee refused	28	78	35	92
Detainee in custody for short time only	3	8	0	0
Custody staff thought it inappropriate	2	6	0	0
Interviewed by researcher previously	3	8	0	0
Other	0	0	3	8
Missing	1	-	2	-
Total	37	100	40	100

Table A.6 Reasons for not obtaining a urine specimen from detainees interviewed

	Nottingham		Sunderland	
Total interviewed	209		271	
Total interviews with specimens	132		210	
Total interviews without specimens	77		61	
Reasons for not collecting a specimen	n	Valid % (exc. missing)	n	Valid % (exc. missing)
Detainee refused	53	82	35	66
Detainee tried, but was unsuccessful	12	19	18	34
Missing	12	-	8	-
Total	77	101	61	100

The next table in this appendix compares detainees who provided a specimen with those who did not. Table A.7 shows that there was a significant difference between those who provided a specimen and those who did not in terms of sex and race. Female interviewees were significantly less likely than male interviewees to provide a specimen (76 per cent of males and 61 per cent of females provided a urine sample). Non-white respondents were also significantly less likely than white respondents to provide a specimen (75 per cent of white respondents and 64 per cent of non-white respondents provided a urine sample). The final section of the table also shows that there is a significant difference between detainees who provide a specimen and those who do not in terms of recent drug use. It was estimated at the beginning of the project that drug users would be less likely to provide a specimen than non-drug users, because they would know that their drug use would be detected. In fact, the results show the opposite to be the case. Arrestees who provided a specimen were significantly more likely than those who did not to report recent drug use. This finding fits anecdotal information provided by the researchers who thought that arrestees who did not provide a urine specimen were generally meeker and milder than their counterparts who did provide a specimen.

These biases have less impact on the results of the study than might at first be expected. The results presented in Table A.1 show that there was no significant difference between the specimen sample and the population in relation to sex. Nevertheless, in all comparisons the percentage of females in the specimen sample was lower than the percentage of females in the populations. The results presented in Table A.1 also show that there was a significant difference in terms of race between the specimen and population samples in two of the five study areas. However, in three of the study areas there was no significant difference.

The main issue of concern is the possible effect that any bias in the specimen sample might have on the urinalysis results. It is important that the prevalence results shown in this part of the analysis are fairly representative of the population of arrestees from which they are drawn. In order to estimate the effect of the specimen sample bias on the drug use prevalence results generated by the urinalysis (specimen sample bias will not, of course, affect the self-report drug use results) the specimen sample was weighted to match more closely the interview sample in terms of sex, race, and self-reported drug use in the last three days. The results of this analysis are shown in Table A.8 below.

Table A.7 A comparison of arrestees who gave a urine specimen with those who did not give a urine specimen
Percentages

	Specimen n=621	No specimen n=218
Sex		
Males	76	24 ***
Females	61	39
Age		
16-20	75	25
21-30	72	28
31 or more	78	22
Race		
White	75	25 **
Non-white	64	36
One or more drug types used		
Used in the last 3 days	79	21 ***
Not used in the last 3 days	68	33

Notes: *=p<.05; **p<.01; ***=p<.001; ns=not significant.

Table A.8 Percentage positive tests among arrestees for selected drug types after weighting for differences in the specimen and interview samples in terms of sex, race, and in self-reported drug use in the last three days
Percentages

	Unweighted results	Weighted to adjust for sex differences	Weighted to adjust for race differences	Weighted to adjust for differences in self-reported drug use over the last 3 days
Alcohol	25	25	25	25
Amphetamines	11	11	10	10
Benzodiazepines	12	12	12	12
Cannabis	46	46	47	44
Cocaine	10	10	10	9
LSD	0	0	0	0
Methadone	8	8	8	7
Opiates	18	19	18	18

Table A.8 shows the unweighted prevalence results for positive drug tests as presented earlier in the report. The remaining columns show the percentage of positive tests among arrestees after adjusting for specimen sample bias. In effect, the specimen sample was weighted to match the distribution of the interview sample in terms of sex, race, and self-reported recent drug use. The table shows that there is little change in the results obtained. Adjusting the specimen sample in terms of sex had the effect of increasing the percentage of arrestees in the total sample from 18 per cent to 19 per cent who tested positive for opiates. This is because females were consistently more likely than males to test positive for opiates across all research sites. Nevertheless, the impact on the findings as a whole was small. Adjusting the specimen sample in terms of race showed a one percentage point decrease in the number of positive tests for amphetamines overall and a one percentage point increase in the number of positive tests for cannabis. This also reflected the tendency for non-white arrestees to be more likely than white arrestees to test positive for cannabis and less likely to test positive for amphetamines. Adjusting the specimen sample in terms of self-reported recent drug use showed a reduction of one percentage point in terms of positive tests for amphetamines, cocaine, and methadone, and a reduction of two percentage points in terms of positive tests for cannabis. This finding reflects the tendency for arrestees less involved in drug use to be less likely to provide a specimen.

Overall, the specimen sample was very similar to the interview sample and the differences that were observed tended to have only a small effect on the percentage of positive tests recorded. Hence, it is proposed that the prevalence figures shown earlier in the report represent the population of arrestees fairly well. However, these one or two percentage point variations need to be taken into account when evaluating the findings and would need to be taken into account when making comparisons across areas and over time.

—

Appendix B: Urinalysis versus self-report measures of drug use

One of the main reasons for developing drug testing of arrestees in the United States was the belief that offenders would not be truthful in admitting drug use during an interview. Subsequent analysis of the results of self-reported drug use and urine testing results has tended to confirm this belief. The evidence from the United States suggests that arrestees who tested positive for drugs substantially under-report drug use (Decker, 1992).

It is possible to compare self-reported drug use as reported in the interview (specifically over the last three days or last month) with the results of the urine analysis found for the same arrestees. The results are shown in the following table.

Figure B.1 A comparison of self-reported drug use three days before arrest and the results of the urinalysis: n=621

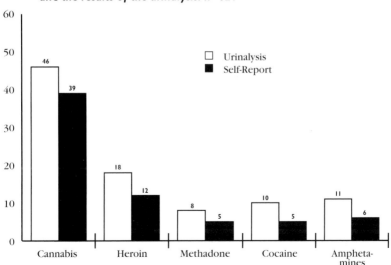

Note: The comparison shown as 'heroin' comprises a comparison of the proportion of positive tests for 'opiates' compared with the proportion of respondents admitting 'heroin' use in the last three days.

The figure shows the percentage of respondents who tested positive for each of the selected drugs and the percentage of the same arrestees who admitted using the selected drugs in the last three days. For example, 62 (10%) of the 621 arrestees who provided a urine specimen tested positive for cocaine, whereas only 32 of these (5% of the 621 arrestees) reported cocaine or crack use in the last three days. However, it should be noted that there may be a number of reasons for the disparity between the results of the self-reported drug use and the results of the urinalysis, including the effect of consuming prescribed or over-the-counter drugs in relation to opiates and amphetamines (see Appendix C) and the effect of the relatively long half-life in relation to cannabis. Nevertheless, the disparity in relation to cocaine is much less likely to be the result of these two effects.

The research was also able to test, to a limited extent, the possible level of over-reporting of drug use. This was done by including a fictitious drug (semeron) within the list of self-reported drug types. The main aim of including this drug was to detect 'yea-saying', or the possibility that respondents will simply say, 'yes' to everything in a list of similar questions without proper thought. The results showed that eight (1%) of the 839 arrestees interviewed said that they had taken semeron at some time in their lives. Four arrestees (0.5%) said that they had consumed semeron in the last year, three (0.4%) in the last month, and one (0.1%) in the last three days. While any errors of this kind are of concern, the level of error (especially in relation to recent drug use) is very small. If anything, the results add confidence to the results by showing that respondents were able to identify drugs which they had not consumed with some accuracy (at least 99% of all responses given in relation to semeron were true negatives).

Appendix C: The effect of prescribed and over-the-counter drugs on the urinalysis results

It was mentioned in Chapter Two that one of the problems of the KIMS test and other screening tests based on urinalysis was the possibility of cross-reactivity, whereby other substances, apart from the drugs being investigated, produce a positive result. This is a particular problem in relation to the current findings relating to opiates. The urinalysis results show a relatively high proportion of arrestees test positive for opiates. However, it is unknown what proportion of these were a result of the consumption of heroin or the consumption of common codeine-based painkillers which might also produce a positive result. While it is not possible to determine these proportions exactly without conducting a confirmatory test (which was not done during the research), it is possible to estimate the proportions from additional information obtained during the interviews.

The results of this analysis are shown in Table C.1. The table shows the proportion of all arrestees who tested positive for opiates who reported using heroin and other illegal opiates during the three days before interview and who reported using legally-prescribed or over-the-counter opiates in the three days before interview. The category of 'other opiates' includes only DF118's as this was the only other opiate among the drug types included in the questionnaire that might generate a positive test for opiates on the particular screening test used.

It was reported earlier that 18 per cent of arrestees who provided a urine specimen tested positive for opiates (114 of 621 or 18.4%). The results shown in the table can be used to produce various estimates of the proportion of arrestees who tested positive for opiates who might have consumed heroin.

Table C.1 Use of legally prescribed and over-the-counter drugs and illegal opiates among arrestees testing positive for opiates

Urinalysis sample n=621 Positive for opiates n=114	Use of legally prescribed or over-the-counter opium-based drugs in the last 3 days [1]			
Use of illegal opiates in the last 3 days	Used (identity of drug known)	Used (identity of drug unknown) [2]	Did not use	Total
Heroin (alone or in combination with other opiates) [3]	(A) 4 (5)	(B) 1 (1)	(C) 68 (90)	73
Other opiates (excluding heroin) [3]	(D) 1 (1)	(E) 1 (1)	(F) 0 (0)	2
No opiates	(G) 2 (3)	(H) 9 (12)	(I) 28 (0)	39
Total	7	11	96	114

Notes: [1] Figures in round brackets represent the estimates of actual cell frequencies when cell I frequencies (which are likely to be the product of concealment of consumption of legal or illegal opiates) are redistributed proportionately to other cells in the table.
[2] These all comprised reports of 'painkillers' (unspecified).
[3] 'Other opiates' include only DF118's, as this was the only drug (in addition to heroin) discussed in the interview which was able to trigger a positive test for opiates.

Likelihood that the positive test detected recent heroin use:

Cell	Probability
C	= high probability
B	= fairly high probability
A	= fairly high probability
D to H	= low probability
I	= possible concealment of consumption of either legal or illegal opiates

The 28 responses shown for arrestees who tested positive for opiates, but who did not report any legal or illegal opiate use in the last three days, is most likely to be explained by concealment of use (and less likely to be explained by the use of some very unusual opiate rarely used legally or illegally). Estimates calculated on the existing distribution of responses would be biased by the inclusion of responses in this cell. More realistic estimates can be obtained by redistributing the responses in this cell proportionately (in accordance with existing cell percentages) to the remaining cells. The following estimates are based on these adjusted figures.

The cell frequencies on which they are based are shown in the table in round brackets.

Original prevalence of positive tests for opiates

=114/621=18.4%

High probability that the test detected heroin use (cell C only)

=90/621=14.5%

Fairly high probability that the test detected heroin use (cells B and C)

=91/621=14.7%

Fairly high probability that the test detected heroin use (cells A, B and C)

=96/621=15.5%

The best estimate of the proportion of all positive tests for opiates which involved heroin (alone or in combination with other drugs) is 15.5% (16% when rounded).

Appendix D: Supplementary tables

Table D.1 Percentage positive tests among arrestees by sex and by location

	Sunder-land	Notting-ham	Cam-bridge	London	Man-chester
Cannabis					
Males	37	48 ***	57	57	61
Females	31	13	38	17	38
Opiates					
Males	13	16	18	18	29
Females	15	17	50	50	63
Methadone					
Males	2	7	7	8 *	19 *
Females	0	0	13	50	63
Cocaine					
Males	1 *	11	3	26	25
Females	8	4	13	33	50
Amphetamines					
Males	8	13	17	0 ***	9
Females	15	13	0	33	13
Benzodiazepines					
Males	11	6	11	14	23
Females	8	9	0	33	38
Alcohol					
Males	44	25	11	24	9
Females	31	13	0	0	0
Multiple Drugs [1]					
Males	31	31	35	39	43
Females	31	13	50	67	63
Any Drug [1]					
Males	74	76	73	82	80
Females	69	52	50	83	88
n=					
Males	183	109	115	72	69
Females	26	23	8	6	8
Total	209	132	123	78	77

Notes: [1] Includes alcohol.
   * p<.05; ** p<.01; ***p<.001 (Chi-squared test: corrected for 2X2 tables). Cells without any of the above symbols were either 'not significant' (p>.05) or 'not applicable' (certain conditions of the Chi-squared test were not met).

Table D.2 Percentage positive tests among arrestees by age and by location

	Sunder-land	Notting-ham	Cam-bridge	London	Man-chester
Cannabis					
16-20	40	53	57	77 *	76
21-30	38	38	57	57	56
31 or more	27	37	52	36	50
Opiates					
16-20	9	9	7 ***	9	19
21-30	18	19	35	30	39
31 or more	10	17	11	21	33
Methadone					
16-20	0	6	0	0	10
21-30	4	5	11	17	28
31 or more	0	9	11	15	28
Cocaine					
16-20	0	3	0	14 *	14
21-30	4	11	6	48	36
31 or more	0	14	4	21	28
Amphetamines					
16-20	7	12	12	0	0
21-30	12	14	17	4	17
31 or more	8	11	22	3	6
Benzodiazepines					
16-20	9	3	5	0	19
21-30	14	8	11	17	33
31 or more	6	9	19	24	17
Alcohol					
16-20	43	18	10	14 **	5
21-30	35	21	4	4	3
31 or more	55	31	26	39	22
Multiple Drugs [1]					
16-20	25	18	24	23	24
21-30	37	30	41	52	56
31 or more	29	34	44	45	50
Any Drug [1]					
16-20	72	79	67	86	86
21-30	76	65	74	83	81
31 or more	71	77	78	79	78
n=					
16-20	75	34	42	22	21
21-30	84	63	54	23	36
31 or more	49	35	27	33	18
Total	208	132	123	78	75

Notes: [1] Includes alcohol. * p<.05; ** p<.01; ***p<.001. Cells without any of the above symbols were either 'not significant' (p>.05) or 'not applicable' (certain conditions of the Chi-squared test were not met).

Table D.3 Percentage positive tests among arrestees by ethnic group and by location

	Sunder-land	Notting-ham	Cam-bridge	London	Man-chester
Cannabis					
White	36	41	56	36 *	59
Non-white	0	43	46	68	67
Opiates					
White	13	17	21	25	33
Non-white	0	0	15	18	33
Methadone					
White	1	7	9	14	24
Non-white	0	0	0	8	17
Cocaine					
White	1	10	5	22	29
Non-white	0	14	0	30	17
Amphetamines					
White	9	13	21	8	10
Non-white	0	0	0	0	0
Benzodiazepines					
White	11	8	14	19	26
Non-white	0	0	0	8	17
Alcohol					
White	43	24	12	31	7
Non-white	50	14	8	15	0
Multiple Drugs [1]					
White	31	29	42	33	47
Non-white	0	14	8	43	33
Any Drug [1]					
White	74	73	73	86	80
Non-white	50	57	61	78	83
n=					
White	207	120	86	36	70
Non-white	2	7	13	40	6
Total	209	127	99	76	76

Notes: [1] Includes alcohol.
* p<.05; ** p<.01; ***p<.001 (Chi-squared test: corrected for 2X2 tables). Cells without any of the above symbols were either 'not significant' (p>.05) or 'not applicable' (certain conditions of the Chi-squared test were not met).

Table D.4 Percentage positive tests among arrestees by offence type and by location

	Sunder-land	Notting-ham	Cam-bridge	London	Man-chester
Cannabis					
Property	43	39	51	64	63
Person	33	46	60	30	71
Alcohol/drugs	27	46	86	54	0
Disorder	22	25	67	50	67
Opiates					
Property	17	23	23	23	35
Person	22	15	16	10	14
Alcohol/drugs	5	0	14	31	0
Disorder	6	0	0	25	0
Methadone					
Property	4	9	11	18	20
Person	0	0	4	0	29
Alcohol/drugs	0	0	0	0	0
Disorder	0	0	0	25	0
Cocaine					
Property	2	13	6	36	29
Person	0	15	0	10	14
Alcohol/drugs	0	8	0	23	0
Disorder	0	0	0	13	0
Amphetamines					
Property	10	10	24	3	8
Person	11	8	4	0	0
Alcohol/drugs	14	39	0	8	0
Disorder	0	25	0	0	33
Benzodiazepines					
Property	16	5	11	23	27
Person	7	23	12	10	14
Alcohol/drugs	9	0	14	8	0
Disorder	9	0	0	13	0
Alcohol					
Property	34 ***	25	13	13	6
Person	44	23	4	40	0
Alcohol/drugs	91	46	14	8	100
Disorder	59	50	0	50	67

Table D.4 *Percentage positive tests among arrestees by offence type and by location (continued)*

	Sunder-land	Notting-ham	Cam-bridge	London	Man-chester
Multiple Drugs [1]					
Property	40	35	43	49	49
Person	30	23	24	20	29
Alcohol/drugs	36	31	29	31	0
Disorder	22	25	0	50	33
Any Drug [1]					
Property	73	72	73	87	84
Person	69	85	64	70	86
Alcohol/drugs	100	100	100	85	0
Disorder	72	75	67	88	0
n= [2]					
Property	82	57	25	10	7
Person [3]	27	13	70	39	49
Alcohol/drugs	22	13	7	13	1
Disorder	32	4	3	8	3
Other/not applicable	46	45	19	9	17
Total [4]	209	132	124	79	77

Notes: [1] Includes alcohol.

* p<.05; ** p<.01; ***p<.001. Cells without any of the above symbols were either 'not significant' (p>.05) or 'not applicable' (certain conditions of the Chi-squared test were not met).

[2] The classification of offences into the groups shown is discussed in Chapter 3. Arrestees who did not provide a urine specimen, who were not held under suspicion of commission of an offence, or who were held for other offences, were excluded from this analysis.

[3] Includes robbery and theft person.

[4] Total sums to 621.

Table D.5 Percentage positive tests among arrestees by main offence type

	Cannabis	Opiates	Meth-adone	Cocaine	Amphet-amines	Benzo-diazepines	Alcohol	% of offences with pos. test	Total offences (a) [1]	Total offences (b) [2]
Murder	50	50	0	0	0	0	0	100	2	4
GBH	50	17	8	0	8	17	17	75	12	14
ABH	31	23	8	4	4	15	38	77	26	37
Wounding	0	0	0	0	0	0	0	0	1	2
Assault (other)	100	0	0	50	50	0	0	100	2	4
Sex Off. (inc. rape)	100	0	0	0	0	0	0	100	1	1
Sex Off. (ind. ass)	0	100	0	0	0	0	0	100	1	2
Sex Off. (other)	50	0	0	0	0	0	0	50	2	3
Burglary (dwelling)	71	11	0	0	14	11	26	80	35	39
Burglary (non-dwelling)	52	28	8	4	20	24	16	76	25	29
Burglary (unspecified)	67	17	0	17	0	0	17	83	6	7
Robbery	58	5	0	5	11	11	32	68	19	25
Offensive weapon	33	0	0	0	0	0	33	33	3	3
Theft (person)	58	25	0	8	0	8	0	58	12	16
Theft (dwelling)	100	0	0	0	0	0	0	100	1	3
Theft (employee)	0	25	0	0	0	0	25	50	4	5
Theft (cycle)	60	0	0	20	0	0	0	60	5	7
Theft (from veh.)	56	11	6	11	0	11	6	78	18	26
Theft (of veh.)	42	23	12	15	31	12	19	81	26	30
Theft (TWOC)	73	9	0	9	18	27	36	91	11	15
Theft (shops)	43	47	29	30	8	20	12	80	90	128
Theft (machine)	67	0	0	0	0	0	0	67	3	3
Theft (other)	47	13	7	13	13	13	33	73	15	17
Handling	0	0	0	0	0	0	0	0	1	4

									Total (a)	Total (b)
Fraud (deception)	45	5	0	5	18	9	0	45	22	30
Arson	33	0	0	0	0	67	33	100	3	4
Criminal damage	49	6	0	3	6	11	46	80	35	41
Drugs (supply)	44	44	0	0	33	22	11	100	9	13
Drugs (possession)	74	11	0	16	21	0	11	89	19	31
Drugs (production)	100	0	0	0	50	0	0	100	1	1
Going equipped	50	0	0	0	0	0	50	100	2	4
POA (S.2) vi.dis.	0	0	0	0	0	0	0	0	7	8
POA (S.3) affray	75	0	0	0	0	0	25	100	4	4
POA (S.4) pr. vi.	25	0	0	0	0	0	50	75	4	6
POA (other)	42	25	8	8	0	17	67	92	12	14
Threats (to kill)	67	0	0	0	0	0	33	100	3	3
Threats (other)	0	0	0	0	0	100	0	100	1	2
Begging	50	25	0	25	0	25	50	75	4	4
Breach of peace	30	10	10	5	0	15	75	90	20	29
Disq. driving	41	18	9	18	9	9	5	59	22	27
RTA	100	0	0	0	0	0	100	100	1	4
Drunkenness	25	0	0	0	10	10	90	100	20	28
Non-payment fine	100	100	0	0	100	0	0	100	1	2
Prostitution (related)	33	0	0	0	0	0	0	33	3	7
Disorderly beh.	50	0	0	0	17	0	17	67	6	6
Breath test/drink dri.	0	0	0	0	0	0	100	100	5	9
Other	34	26	11	3	6	9	11	60	35	53
Missing	*	*	*	*	*	*	*	*	61	85
Total	*	*	*	*	*	*	*	*	621	839

Notes: [1] Total offences (a)=offences relating only to those arrestees who provided a urine specimen.
[2] Total offences (b)=Offences relating to all arrestees interviewed.
All percentages are based on 'Total offences (a)'.

Appendix E: Self-reported sources of illegal income

It could be argued that the relationship between self-reported drug use and illegal income was a result of the fact that arrestees who were involved in drug use were also involved in drug sales. If all illegal income were generated from drug sales, then the drugs-crime connection would be wholly a product of drug use and the commission of this one offence. If no illegal income were generated from drug sales then the drugs-crime connection would be wholly a product of drug use and the commission of other income-generating crimes.

One way of testing this proposition is to determine the proportion of all offences committed by arrestees which were drug sales offences or other offences. Information about self-reported offending was collected only in relation to arrestees interviewed in Sunderland. Arrestees were asked to state which of 10 income-generating offences they had committed in the last 12 months (including drug sales). One-hundred-and-forty-eight of the 272 arrestees interviewed in Sunderland said that they had committed none of the listed offences in the last 12 months and have been excluded from the following analysis. The amount of illegal income reported and the type of offences reported for the remainder are shown in Table E.1.

The table shows that only six per cent of respondents reported drug sales as their only income-generating crime in the last 12 months. Fifteen per cent of arrestees reported drugs sales and other offences. Eighty per cent of arrestees reported committing only non-drug sales income-generating offences in the last 12 months. A similar comparison can be made by looking at the proportion of total illegal income generated from drugs sales only or from other offences. At least two-thirds (65%) of all illegal income reported by these arrestees resulted from non-drug sales offences.

Hence, the results do not support the contention that the major proportion of illegal income earned by arrestees was a result of selling drugs. The results also do not support the argument that the correlations shown in the report between drug use and illegal income are largely a product of the fact that drug users obtain illegal income primarily from drug sales. In fact, the analysis suggests the opposite: illegal income is largely a product of the commission of non-drug sales income-generating crimes.

Table E.1 Self-reported illegal income over the last 12 months by type of offences committed: Sunderland

Self-reported offences	Total cases	% of total cases	Total illegal income (across all cases in each category)	% of total illegal income
	n	%	£	%
Drug supply offences only	7	6	114,000	12
Drug supply offences with other offences	18	15	225,660	23
Other offences only	98	80	623,989	65
Total	123	101	963,649	100

Notes: The table excludes 148 cases in which the arrestee reported committing none of the 10 listed offences in the last 12 months. One further case had no information on illegal income and was classified as missing.

Publications

List of research publications

A list of research reports for the last year is provided below. A **full** list of publications is available on request from the Research and Statistics Directorate Information and Publications Group.

Home Office Research Studies (HORS)

170. **Understanding the sentencing of women.** Edited by Carol Hedderman and Lorraine Gelsthorpe. 1997.

171. **Changing offenders' attitudes and behaviour: what works?** Julie Vennard, Darren Sugg and Carol Hedderman 1997.

172. **Drug misuse declared in 1996: latest results from the British Crime Survey.** Malcolm Ramsay and Josephine Spiller. 1997.

173. **Ethnic monitoring in police forces: a beginning.** Marian FitzGerald and Rae Sibbitt. 1997.

174. **In police custody: Police powers and suspects' rights under the revised PACE codes of practice.** Tom Bucke and David Brown. 1997.

176. **The perpetrators of racial harassment and racial violence.** Rae Sibbitt. 1997.

177. **Electronic monitoring in practice: the second year of the trials of curfew orders.** Ed Mortimer and Chris May. 1997.

179. **Attitudes to punishment: findings from the British Crime Survey.** Michael Hough and Julian Roberts. 1998.

Nos. 175, 178, 180, 181 and 182 are not published yet.

Research Findings

47. **Sentencing without a pre-sentence report**. Nigel Charles, Claire Whittaker and Caroline Ball. 1997.

48. **Magistrates' views of the probation service.** Chris May. 1997.

49. **PACE ten years on: a review of the research.** David Brown. 1997.

50. **Persistent drug–misusing offenders.** Malcolm Ramsay. 1997.

51. **Curfew orders with electronic monitoring: The first twelve months.** Ed Mortimer and George Mair. 1997.

52. **Police cautioning in the 1990s.** Roger Evans and Rachel Ellis. 1997.

53. **A reconviction study of HMP Grendon Therapeutic Community.** Peter Marshall. 1997.

54. **Control in category c prisons.** Simon Marshall. 1997.

55. **The prevalence of convictions for sexual offending.** Peter Marshall. 1997.

56. **Drug misuse declared in 1996: key results from the British Crime Survey.** Malcolm Ramsay and Josephine Spiller. 1997.

57. **The 1996 International Crime Victimisation Survey.** Pat Mayhew and Phillip White. 1997.

58. **The sentencing of women: a section 95 publication.** Carol Hedderman and Lizanne Dowds. 1997.

59. **Ethnicity and contacts with the police: latest findings from the British Crime Survey.** Tom Bucke. 1997.

60. **Policing and the public: findings from the 1996 British Crime Survey.** Catriona Mirrlees-Black and Tracy Budd. 1997.

61. **Changing offenders' attitudes and behaviour: what works?** Julie Vennard, Carol Hedderman and Darren Sugg. 1997.

62. **Suspects in police custody and the revised PACE codes of practice.** Tom Bucke and David Brown. 1997.

63. **Neighbourhood watch co-ordinators.** Elizabeth Turner and Banos Alexandrou. 1997.

64. **Attitudes to punishment: findings from the 1996 British Crime Survey.** Michael Hough and Julian Roberts. 1998.

65. **The effects of video violence on young offenders.** Kevin Browne and Amanda Pennell. 1998.

66. **Electronic monitoring of curfew orders: the second year of the trials.** Ed Mortimer and Chris May. 1998.

67. **Public perceptions of drug-related crime in 1997.** Nigel Charles. 1998.

68. **Witness care in magistrates' courts and the youth court.** Joyce Plotnikoff and Richard Woolfson. 1998.

Occasional Papers

Evaluation of a Home Office initiative to help offenders into employment. Ken Roberts, Alana Barton, Julian Buchanan and Barry Goldson. 1997.

The impact of the national lottery on the horse-race betting levy. Simon Field and James Dunmore. 1997.

The cost of fires. A review of the information available. Donald Roy. 1997.

Monitoring and evaluation of WOLDS remand prison and comparisons with public-sector prisons, in particular HMP Woodhill. A Keith Bottomley, Adrian James, Emma Clare and Alison Liebling. 1997.

Requests for Publications

Home Office Research Studies and, Research Findings can be requested from:

Research and Statistics Directorate
Information and Publications Group
Room 201, Home Office
50 Queen Anne's Gate
London SW1H 9AT
Telephone: 0171-273 2084
Fascimile: 0171-222 0211
Internet: http://www.open.gov.uk/home_off/rsd/rsdhome.htm
E-mail: rsd.ha apollo @ gtnet.gov.u.

Occasional Papers can be purchased from:
Home Office
Publications Unit
50 Queen Anne's Gate
London SW1H 9AT
Telephone: 0171-273 2302

HMSO Publications Centre

(Mail, fax and telephone orders only)
PO Box 276, London SW8 5DT
Telephone orders: 0171-873 9090
General enquiries: 0171-873 0011
(queuing system in operation for both numbers)
Fax orders: 0171-873 8200